ENGAGED LEADERSHIP

*Building a Culture to Overcome
Employee Disengagement*

SECOND EDITION

CLINT SWINDALL

WILEY

John Wiley & Sons, Inc.

Published by John Wiley & Sons, Inc., Hoboken, New Jersey.

Published simultaneously in Canada.

For general information on our other products and services or for technical support, please contact our Customer Care Department within the United States at (800) 762-2974, outside the United States at (317) 572-3993, or fax (317) 572-4002.

Wiley also publishes its books in a variety of electronic formats. Some content that appears in print may not be available in electronic books. For more information about Wiley products, visit our web site at www.wiley.com.

Library of Congress Cataloging-in-Publication Data:

Swindall, Clint, 1967–
Engaged leadership: building a culture to overcome employee disengagement/Clint Swindall.—2nd ed.
    p. cm.
  Includes index.
ISBN 978-0-470-93311-4 (cloth)
ISBN 978-1-118-03375-3 (ebk)
ISBN 978-1-118-03376-0 (ebk)
ISBN 978-1-118-03377-7 (ebk)
  1. Leadership. 2. Employee motivation. I. Title.
  HD57.7.S95 2007
  658.4'092—dc22   2010047261

Printed in the United States of America

10 9 8 7 6 5 4 3 2 1

To the two most important women in my life . . .

My mother, Sherron Hartin,
whose unselfish sacrifices to send me to college
paved the way for my experiences in corporate
America. God bless you Mom, for all you are.

To my wife, Heather Swindall,
whose unconditional love and support of
my career give me all the reason I need to
pursue my passion of enhancing the
lives of those around me.

CONTENTS

INTRODUCTION   I

   The Format   11

THE FABLE   15

EPILOGUE   ONE YEAR LATER   145

THE APPLICATION OF ENGAGED LEADERSHIP   155

DIRECTIONAL LEADERSHIP   161

   Challenge One
   Recruit Support from the Top 29 Percent   165

   Challenge Two
   Prepare the Organization for Change   167

   Challenge Three
   Let Them Know How They Contribute   170

   Challenge Four
   Constantly Communicate Progress   174

MOTIVATIONAL LEADERSHIP   177

Challenge Five
Lead with Positive Motivation   180

Challenge Six
Celebrate Small Successes   183

Challenge Seven
Encourage Life Balance for All Employees   186

Challenge Eight
Create a Fair Work Environment   190

ORGANIZATIONAL LEADERSHIP   193

Challenge Nine
Identify and Position the Appropriate Talent   195

Challenge Ten
Build a Bridge between Generations   198

Challenge Eleven
Move toward Real Empowerment   200

Challenge Twelve
Establish a Strategy to Maintain Success   202

THE IMPORTANCE OF CHARACTER CORE   205

CONCLUSION   209

THE EMPLOYEE'S ROLE   211

Acknowledgments   214

About the Author   217

Introduction

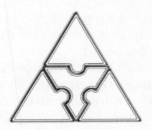

When *Engaged Leadership* was first published in 2007, the challenge of overcoming employee disengagement was significant. With research showing that three-quarters of employees in any organization were at some level of disengagement, the need to overcome the epidemic of employee disengagement was very real. As a professional speaker, I had shared my thoughts with tens of thousands of people on this topic for years. As an author, I considered it a privilege to reach even more people with *Engaged Leadership*.

These past four years have been exciting as I've traveled the world sharing the model of *Engaged Leadership*. It has been thrilling to see the success of the book. But even more than that, it has been extremely rewarding to see the application of ideas shared in the book. Whether working with a client as a consultant or having a conversation with someone halfway around the world who read the book, it has been humbling to hear that *Engaged*

Leadership is helping leaders discover how to build a culture to overcome employee disengagement.

While witnessing the success of the book over the past four years may have been exciting, watching the impact of the downturn in the economy was far from exciting. As organizations scrambled to survive the recession, the lives of employees were changed. Unemployment was on the rise, and the impact was widespread.

Some felt the direct hit of a pink slip. With unemployment hovering around 10 percent, many people suffered financial hardship from lost income. Perhaps even worse, many became poor in spirit, dealing with the loss of purpose and sense of achievement. The cost associated with unemployment continued to rise with strained relationships. The negative impact of unemployment on the 10 percent who are no longer employed is undeniable.

Throughout these tough times, those people who have remained employed have been considered the "lucky" ones. Although they may have escaped layoffs from downsizing, they have suffered the impact of being left behind. In many cases, remaining employees have been asked to do the work of two or three people. Quite often they are expected to accomplish this arduous task with no increase in pay (or they may even be asked to take a pay cut). Budget cuts have all but eliminated training opportunities, so professional development often has been put on hold. In some cases, significant emotional and psychological trauma has resulted from seeing a close friend or peer let go. Because of the fear and uncertainty of when the recession will end, many leaders have stopped communicating as regularly with employees; this causes even greater fear and uncertainty among employees. As a result, the still-employed "lucky" ones may be left wondering if the next pink slip will have their name on it.

So, what has been the impact on the employees left behind? Have they become more engaged, hoping their increased engagement will allow them to survive any further cuts? Have they become less engaged, allowing the desperation of the recession to bring them down? Well, it depends what research you believe.

According to Gallup polls conducted since *Engaged Leadership* was first published in 2007, employee engagement has hardly shifted at all during this recession. A 2010 study conducted by the human resources consulting firm Towers Watson found that employee engagement levels had dropped by nearly 10 percent since the previous year. And according to the Conference Board, a nonprofit global research group, job satisfaction in the United States is at its lowest level in two decades.

These sources are all very reliable. What accounts for the discrepancies in their research findings? There are many possibilities. Could one study be asking more relevant questions than another? Could one study have used a more reliable survey tool? Is some methodological error driving the differences in the data?

Although it can be a fascinating endeavor to parse the data related to employee disengagement, one simple fact will always be indisputable: employee disengagement exists, and we need to be working to create a culture to overcome it. As I work with clients in many industries, I see the disengagement everywhere I go. I don't need a study to convince me it exists.

Before I considered what should be included in a second edition of *Engaged Leadership,* I needed to answer a very basic question: Should employee engagement still be the goal? After all, we've been through a global economic recession since the first edition of this book was released, so maybe business leaders should change their focus. It didn't take much thought to reach the conclusion that employee engagement must continue to be the goal. There are many reasons building a culture of engagement is even more important now than it was four years ago. Here are just a few:

1. The level of productivity of those left behind is often confused with genuine employee engagement. Throughout this recession, I have encountered several people who have indicated the employee engagement in their company is high because the work is getting done and "we're holding our own" during these tough times. In some cases, the work may be getting done because the employee engagement level is high. In other cases I've observed throughout the recession, the work is getting done because those left behind are trying to avoid the next round of job cuts. An employee who comes in early and stays late is not necessarily the sign of an engaged employee. An employee who is doing the work of two or three employees is not necessarily the sign of an engaged employee. As organizations emerge from the downturn in the economy and the fear of job loss subsides, leaders must focus on building a culture of engagement to ensure high levels of productivity.
2. The days of tolerating employee disengagement are gone. When times were great and

organizations had plenty of employees to get the job done, it was rather easy for leaders to over-look disengaged employees. In fact, mediocrity was accepted as long as the organization was meeting its targets. Now that teams are smaller, it is essential that employers get the most from employees. The surest way to maxi-mize employee productivity is to build a culture of engagement.

3. Successful organizations will not settle for going back to where they were before the reces-sion. While some employees (and managers) are waiting for the recession to end so they can get back to the way it used to be, strong leaders are raising the bar and expecting a new "normal" as a result of the recession. They realize that by the time they get back to where they were, the competition will already be heading in a new direction. For companies to compete, they need engaged employees to take them to the new "normal."

4. Employees will have new opportunities when the economy recovers and employers start hir-ing again. For years now, many employees have stayed in poorly led organizations because their options were few. When options become availa-ble again, employees will consider how well they've been treated throughout the recession to determine whether they stay or leave. Also, they'll base their loyalty on how loyal the orga-nization was to them during the tough times. Leaders actively engaged in building a culture of engagement will foster employee loyalty, which will help retain employees when poten-tial opportunities arise elsewhere.

5. Some companies will never hire at previous lev-els again. Throughout the recession, many cut

their workforce to survive the tough times. In many cases, they cut low performers. As a result, many companies are seeing the same amount of work getting done by fewer people. The best way to ensure that these productive employees who carried the organization through the recession will stay long after the recession is over is to build a culture of engagement.

6. Research shows that organizations that score higher on employee engagement surveys have stronger financial performance. According to a 2010 Gallup poll, organizations that scored in the top 10 percent on employee engagement surveys outperformed their competition by 72 percent in earnings per share during 2007–2008. For organizations that scored beneath the top quartile, earnings fell 9.4 percent below their competition. And according to a Towers Watson poll, companies with high levels of employee engagement outperformed those with less-engaged employees in operating income, net income growth rate, and earnings-per-share growth rate.

If these reasons aren't enough to persuade business leaders of the continued importance of building a culture of engagement, consider this. There often is a disconnect between the leader's perception of employee engagement and the employee's perception of employee engagement. Regardless of the strength of an organization, the view of employee engagement (and how that ties to the overall culture of the organization) always differs between the boardroom and the break room. After more than a decade of working with clients, I have found the engagement of employees is never as high as the leaders believe it is.

With that in mind, what would employees say about the culture of your organization? Let's say your company is emerging from the recession. There's a position you've needed to fill for quite some time, and the hiring freeze is over and you've been given the green light to fill the position. You've interviewed several qualified candidates, and after sharing with each candidate the wonderful culture of your organization, you've narrowed your search to one final candidate. You've made the offer, but before the person will accept, she's asked to have a quick meeting with a group of randomly selected employees.

"It's no big deal," she says. "I just want to hear what they have to say about the organization, and where they think the company's headed. I'd like to get an idea about what it's like to work here." She may say it's no big deal, but you know her decision hinges on what she hears in this meeting.

As you wait anxiously in your office for the outcome, questions fly through your head: "What are they saying about the company? What are they saying about our future? What are they saying about our values? What are they saying about my leadership team? What are they saying about *me*?"

Chances are, once you answer each of these questions in your head, you then ask the most important question of all. "Do I fire them all when they get out, or just a few?"

Some of you holding this book may very well need oxygen if you were to really think about how your employees might answer the questions of a prospective employee. The amount of oxygen you would need quite possibly depends on how well you took care of your employees throughout the economic downturn.

On the other hand, some of you wouldn't be concerned at all if a prospective employee were to ask for a meeting with current employees. You'd take a leisurely walk down to the closest coffee shop for your morning coffee, knowing your team is giving you and your organization a glowing review. Why? Because you know your employees have a high commitment to the organization and its values. You know your employees are dedicated to the vision and are eager to contribute. You know they are bragging about how productive the team is, and how the leaders of the organization live by the organization's values. In fact, they are bragging about how well you treated them throughout the recession, while other companies put profits first and employees second. In a nutshell, you know you have engaged employees.

Before you take that first sip of your hazelnut cappuccino, you may want to sit down. According to research, most employees don't fit that description. In fact, according to the most recent survey conducted by the Gallup Organization, only 29 percent of employees are engaged. It's a sad fact, but the majority (71 percent) of employees were found to be disengaged: 54 percent "disengaged" and 17 percent "actively disengaged." They show up to work each day and do the minimum to get by. They collect a paycheck and go home. These aren't bad people. They simply don't have a passion for their work, and they make up more than half of any organization's workforce.

The Gallup poll found that the remaining 17 percent of employees are what can be called "actively" disengaged. These employees are not committed to the organization's future and are opposed to just about everything you do. Most are miserable, and want to share it with anyone who will listen. In fact, they're out recruiting new members of this actively disengaged group every day. And in some cases, they are the most vocal and influential leaders in the organization.

Based on these statistics from the Gallup survey, there's a good chance your job candidate is getting an earful of something you'd rather she not hear. With only one of every four employees truly engaged on the job, it wouldn't be surprising.

The problem of employee disengagement is a source of ongoing frustration for leaders of any organization. Not only does it irritate the management team, it demoralizes the productive employees who carry most of the workload. And although employee disengagement exists, what is really being done to overcome it?

My experience has shown me that most leaders just complain about employee disengagement. Even worse, they find a way to blame it on the employee. "They're just lazy," I hear. "They must be part of that young, unmotivated generation." There seems to be a myriad of excuses why employee disengagement is allowed to continue.

Although employees do have a responsibility to contribute to a culture of employee engagement, business leaders should not attribute to employees the power to overcome disengagement. Leaders who wait and hope an employee will simply "see the light" and suddenly become a productive part of the workforce will wait a long, disappointing time. The responsibility for productivity and profitability rests entirely on the shoulders of leadership, and so does the responsibility to overcome employee disengagement. So, why do so many leaders ignore this responsibility?

There are several reasons, but perhaps the most significant is that most leaders are spending more time managing tasks and not nearly enough time leading people. If you don't believe that observation, just spend one day without your cell phone, PDA, or e-mail. You'll find out quickly how much of your day is spent managing the business and putting out fires rather than leading the people on your team.

There's no doubt that employee disengagement continues to be of major concern, but there is good news. Employees don't want to be disengaged. People start new jobs as engaged employees, hoping to find their productive place. Then something happens. They get a new boss. Their job responsibilities change. Perhaps some promises get broken. We've all been there. The employee faces a fork in the road. He or she either becomes engaged or joins the ranks of disengaged employees.

While we're out running the business, we let employees silently determine which path they'll take when they reach that fork in the road. We learn of their choice when we see a report that shows customer complaints are up or product quality is down. We learn of their choice when we see a report that shows turnover is up or morale is down. It is then that we realize they chose the path of employee disengagement.

The question then is how we help build a culture to overcome employee disengagement. The answer is simple. Employee engagement is a product of strong leadership. In the midst of managing the business, we must focus our efforts on developing better leaders.

The leadership needed today is not any different than it was a hundred years ago. Indeed, the leadership principles we use after the recession don't need to be different than the leadership principles we used before the recession. Most managers have been exposed to numerous approaches to enhance their leadership skills. Many people jump from book to book trying to find new ideas, when the true key to success is to find one single resource that provides the framework for successful leadership and stick with that model. This book provides that model.

And there's even better news. These concepts apply regardless of your role. Whether you run a bank or a small division within a large corporation, the concepts in this book will help you build a culture that will move your business toward employee engagement. Whether you work in a church or lead a nonprofit organization, you will find culture-building ideas that will help you tap into the true potential of your team.

THE FORMAT

Some people absorb every word in a book, either dedicating the time to read the book from cover to cover in one sitting or returning to the book until they reach the end. I have an enormous amount of respect and envy for the discipline and determination of these people.

Although I can scan my bookshelf and identify many great books I enjoyed from cover to cover, I can spot many books I never completed. I heard once that the average reader never gets past the third chapter of a book. I don't know if that's true, but if it is, then I guess I'm not alone.

As a reader, I am comforted by these facts; but as an author, I am distressed. The thought of anyone not getting to the end of my book is disappointing. As a result, the book has been organized to be as inviting as possible to the reader. I use two popular formats that will be familiar and accessible to business leaders: the fable and the how-to.

Many readers are drawn to a fable because people relate to people. They can take the lessons learned in a story and apply them to their own circumstances. In fact, I have found over my years in the professional speaking industry that people have the best chance of learning a concept and actually applying it in their life if they can combine the theory with a real-life example.

Whereas some people are drawn to fables, many readers want to get straight to the point. They want to have the solution spelled out in a direct, how-to format. They need a specific to-do list to feel they have the information they need to put the concepts to work and measure their success.

For those readers who learn from and enjoy a fable, the concepts of *Engaged Leadership* will be introduced through a story. This is not a traditional fable. There are no animals, and the story is told based on real-life challenges in the workplace.

For those readers who want the how-to format, a portion of this book was written just for you. Once you've had a chance to learn the concepts by relating to the characters in the story, specific challenges are provided to help you put those ideas to work.

As I've traveled around speaking about *Engaged Leadership* since it was first released, one of the most common remarks I've heard from people is about the format of the book: *"The book was so easy to read and apply. I learned the lesson in the fable, and got the tools I needed in the how-to portion at the end."* This positive feedback has reinforced the decision to use both methods in the book.

Engaged Leadership has been designed to tap into both sides of your brain. The creative side will benefit from the fable, and the detail side will benefit from the how-to challenges. Whichever way you learn, I encourage you to take the concepts of *Engaged Leadership* and put them to work in your organization as you build a culture to overcome employee disengagement.

Let's start with our fable. The story is about Seth Owen, a young management recruit struggling to understand his role in overcoming employee disengagement. In an office where mediocrity has become an accepted way of life, Seth clashes with fellow managers and employees while attempting to raise the performance bar. With the guidance and encouragement of Hannah Jaxson, a dynamic boss with incredible vision and an uncanny ability to nurture growth in employees, he learns in one year what may take others a lifetime to learn. With Hannah as his mentor, he learns what it takes to build a culture of employee engagement.

The Fable

S eth Owen had it all figured out. He had taken business classes in college, and he assumed managing people wasn't going to be that hard. After all, he thought, his college degree and charismatic personality would make him an ideal boss; employees would love to be on his team.

As he entered the working world as an employee of a Fortune 500 company, Seth was looking forward to putting his degree to work. Although he was an average student in school, Seth was a leader outside the classroom. He had a reputation as the one person you could depend on to get things done. Not only would Seth make things happen as the "go to" guy, he could inspire people around him to help, and he always did it with a smile on his face.

Now that he was out of school, the time for "learning" was over, and the time for "doing" was here. The dress rehearsal had ended. As he headed through the doors of corporate America, Seth had no idea his education was just beginning. Nor did he have any idea that his first year on the job would change the way he viewed business, and life, forever.

THE ARRIVAL

For a small regional airport, there were quite a few people bustling around. As Seth moved through the crowd of departing passengers, he tried to look confident in his new blue suit, freshly starched shirt, cap toe shoes, and yellow tie. He had been told that yellow was a "power" color, and he needed to look powerful that day.

You see, Seth was meeting his new boss. After graduating from college, he spent months looking for a job. The recession limited the number of opportunities available to him and his college buddies, but his wait was finally over and he was going to work for Halifax, a large call center company with offices in central Texas. Despite the recession, this company was growing and had opened a new call center two years earlier just outside of Austin. Seth liked the fact it was a huge company with offices all over the United States. He knew job security was a thing of the past, but he hoped it would be a secure place to be and would provide opportunities for advancement.

Although he had been hired by the corporate recruiting office in New Jersey, Seth was being sent to work in the call center outside Austin. Today was the first time he'd be meeting his new boss, Hannah Jaxson. Seth was eager to meet her because the corporate recruiter had spoken very highly of her. He told Seth she was considered a rising star in the company, and that she was transferred from another department to take over this call center just two months ago.

Seth scanned the crowd as he wandered around the baggage claim area looking for Hannah. He had requested a picture from the corporate recruiter so he would know her when he saw her, but his flight left before he could get the photo. Although he had no idea what Hannah would look like, he had a picture in his mind. She would be tall and confident, have light brown hair, and be well dressed.

As the passengers gathered their luggage and the crowd began to thin, Seth got anxious. He wasn't concerned his new boss wasn't going to be there. He was concerned that maybe he was being tested. He thought to himself, "What if this is part of the test? What if she's standing around the corner watching me wander around lost? Should I have her paged? Should I start approaching any female standing by herself?" If this was a test, he certainly didn't want to fail.

About that time, he heard the page. "Seth Owen. Please meet your party at the baggage claim information desk. Mr. Seth Owen. Please meet your party at the baggage claim information desk."

As he turned to walk that way, he saw a woman emerge from the small crowd around the information desk. Although this woman was waving, this couldn't be her. She didn't even come close to matching the picture he had in his mind. This woman was short and had dark black hair. However, Seth had been half right. Dressed in a dark blue suit, his new boss carried herself with all the confidence in the world.

THE RIDE

It didn't take long for Seth to figure out why Hannah was successful. She was easy to like and had a very charismatic personality. Any anxiety he had was calmed before they got to the car. He had wrongly assumed she would be judging his every move. It quickly became apparent she simply wanted to talk about the job opportunity.

The ride from the airport to the office was just over an hour. Hannah used that time to talk about the assignment. She explained to Seth how she had been given responsibility for this call center just two months ago, and that her biggest challenge so far was shaping the culture. His job experience up to this point had consisted mostly of part-time jobs, so the term "culture" was relatively new to him.

"I'm not sure I know what you mean when you say you're shaping the culture," Seth admitted reluctantly. "Didn't they already have a culture when you got here?"

"They did," Hannah laughed, "but it's a culture that seems to breed mediocrity. Most employees just show up and do the bare minimum to get by, and we have an opportunity to change it. That's a priority for me."

Seth didn't want to seem ignorant to the whole idea of culture, so he didn't press the issue and just looked out the window. Hannah must have sensed his confusion. "Have you ever worked somewhere you didn't like?"

"Yes, I have," Seth responded as he turned from the window. "I worked at a store in a mall. It was awful."

"Tell me what made it so awful," she inquired.

"First of all, my boss treated all the employees like they were inferior. He always yelled at us if we were one minute late for our shift, although he seemed to be late more than anyone."

Hannah asked, "Do you remember the feeling you had when you worked in that environment?"

"Absolutely. It was horrible. I used to hate going to work every day, and I remember what a relief it was when I finally quit."

"That," she said, "is culture. You can't touch it, and you certainly can't explain it in clear terms. It's how people feel when they go to work. My biggest challenge has been convincing my management team we have some work to do in that area."

"Are they not supportive?"

"Let's just say they have some baggage," Hannah said with a smile. "You see, we already have a call center in Austin, about a half hour from our new office. The head of that call center and two of the managers accepted a transfer two years ago when it first opened. The leadership style of my predecessor for nearly two years pretty much ensured a continuation of the old culture."

"Why did your predecessor leave?" Seth asked.

"Early retirement."

Seth asked, "Do you think the employees in this department don't like working at Halifax? Is that why you want to change the culture?"

"That's a fair question. My observation is this office is no different than any other I've had the chance to develop. Most employees are disengaged. They simply show up to work, do the minimum to get by, and collect a paycheck every two weeks. I want to create a culture of employee engagement."

Seth was familiar with Hannah's observation. He had seen employee disengagement at every part-time job he had held up to that point in his life. In fact, there were times he considered himself one of the disengaged. So he asked the most obvious question, "How do you create this culture of employee engagement?"

As they pulled into the parking lot, Hannah looked over and said, "Seth, you have identified the biggest challenge I face every day, and one I hope you can help me work on."

THE MANAGEMENT TEAM

Seth had never been inside a call center before, and didn't really know what to expect. As they entered the office, he was awed with the rows and rows of computer stations all surrounded by low cubicle walls. It was somewhat dark and looked very formal.

Apparently everyone knew Hannah had gone to the airport to get "the new guy." As he glanced around the office, he saw heads popping up over the cubicle walls at each computer station. Seth was prepared to be judged by his new boss, but he hadn't anticipated the scrutiny from the sixty call center reps on duty that morning.

On the ride from the airport, Hannah had explained to Seth that the first order of business would be a meeting in the conference room with the other managers. The office had a total of four managers assigned to manage approximately 100 employees. Seth had asked about his three fellow managers during the ride, but Hannah wouldn't divulge any information. She explained she didn't want to influence his opinion in either direction.

As they entered the conference room right on time, Seth was surprised to see only one person there for the meeting. Hannah had told Seth there was only one male manager, and his name was Aaron King.

Seth had a very aggressive and confident personality, and eagerly approached Aaron before he put down his briefcase.

"You must be Aaron," he said with a smile and an extended hand. "My name is Seth Owen."

"Hello, Seth. I've been looking forward to meeting you. At home I have a wife and three daughters, so I get ganged up on a lot. The same is true for the office. I've been looking forward to some male influence around here!"

Seth was impressed with Aaron. He liked the fact he was on time for the meeting, and he liked his energy.

As they were sitting down, one of the other managers ran into the room. "Sorry I'm late," she said. "I couldn't get one of my employees out of my office." She sat down without saying another word.

Seth stood and reached across the table, extending his hand. "Hi. I'm Seth."

"I'm Jill Ramos," she responded as she tried to catch her breath. "Nice to meet you."

As Seth sat back down, Hannah asked both managers to introduce themselves in more detail. Before either could start, she inquired, "Where's Carmen?"

"She just got on a call with someone from the staff," Jill responded. "She said she would try to make it, but that we shouldn't wait for her."

Without showing too much concern, Hannah looked at Aaron and Jill and asked, "Who wants to go first?"

As if he were expecting the question, Aaron raised his hand and offered to get things started. He explained he had been a manager in the Austin office, and accepted the transfer because this new office was closer to home. Of all the people Seth met that day, he felt the most comfortable around Aaron. He would later learn that Aaron was the manager most employees in the office preferred, and certainly the one most eager to learn about the culture of employee engagement Hannah was trying to put in place.

Jill went next. She started by apologizing again for being late to the meeting. Seth wasn't sure if she was being genuine or just trying to stay out of trouble with Hannah. She explained she had been a call center representative her entire career, and that she got promoted when the new office was opened. She said she was tired of having the least amount of seniority with only two years as a manager, and that she was glad to see a new manager. Seth would later learn that Jill was the most efficient call center representative in the Austin office, and ranked at the top of nearly every area the company measured. He also learned she was struggling with most of the changes Hannah was making to enhance the culture.

After the two other managers had introduced themselves, Seth spent a few minutes sharing his background. As he wrapped up his comments, Hannah explained that she and Seth would meet for the remainder of the afternoon in her office, and that everyone else was welcome to return to work. She turned to Seth and said, "I guess you'll have to meet Carmen at a later time."

Seth didn't know Carmen, but he suspected this was her way of showing she wasn't concerned with "the new guy." Whether his gut feeling was right or not, Seth needed to make a statement of his own. He turned to Hannah and said, "I think I would like to meet her now. Can you take me to her office so I can at least introduce myself?"

Hannah smiled and replied, "I'd be happy to take you to her office." Seth had a feeling he had just earned a little respect from his new boss.

Seth noticed her nameplate as they approached her cubicle. It read "Carmen Fuentes." When they reached her doorway, Carmen spun around in her chair. She wasn't on the telephone, so Seth extended his hand and said, "Hi, my name is Seth Owen. I understand you were on a call this morning during our meeting, so I thought I would stop by and introduce myself. Hannah and I have a meeting, but I wanted to let you know I look forward to working with you."

Not giving Carmen the opportunity to respond, Seth turned back to Hannah and said, "I'm ready when you are!" The two walked across the call center to Hannah's office, where the assessment would begin.

AN ASSESSMENT

As soon as her office door closed, Hannah turned to Seth and asked, "So, what did you think?"

"They all seem to be very nice people," Seth hesitantly replied as he sat down.

Hannah looked at Seth as if she were analyzing his response. "Now that you've provided me the politically correct response, tell me what you really think."

Seth appreciated her openness, but he never had a manager ask his opinion about his fellow employees before. He wondered if this was normal, and was guarded with his response.

"I thought Aaron was pretty sincere. He seems to have an open mind. And Jill seems to be a nice person."

Hannah waited for Seth to continue, and when he didn't elaborate she said, "You're holding back. I want to know what you really think."

Seth sat quietly for a moment, choosing to carefully word his response. He wanted to share his true feelings, but he needed assurance that it was safe to do so.

"Seth," Hannah said as she leaned forward, "I value your judgment. Some bosses would never ask for your honest opinion. However, I believe if a culture of employee engagement is truly going to exist, we must have an environment where honest views are encouraged."

Although Seth wasn't comfortable being critical of anyone he just met, he knew anything short of complete honesty at this point might be seen as a sign of weakness to Hannah, so he shared what was on his mind. "I wasn't terribly impressed with Jill."

"What didn't you like?"

"I'm not sure I can pinpoint it yet," Seth replied. "After her introduction, I just got the feeling she's somewhat insecure. Maybe it's because she hasn't been in management all that long."

"Anyone bother you?"

"Carmen," Seth replied without hesitation.

"What bothered you?"

"Several things," Seth replied. "First, I assume you asked her to be in the meeting."

"I did."

"Well, maybe I'm naïve, but I've always been taught you don't just ignore your boss when she asks you to do something. Beyond the fact it's an act of insubordination, it's just rude. Second, the fact she didn't show up at the meeting sent the message she thinks she's too important to meet her new colleague. That wasn't just a slap to me, but to all the managers. And third, she seemed threatened."

"She is threatened," Hannah said. "Carmen was the queen bee in the Austin office and has continued in that role in this office. She and my predecessor were good friends. In fact, she transferred to this office because she thought she would get promoted when her buddy retired. She's feared by most everyone in the office, and she's been threatened by my style of leadership since I got here."

"How is your style different from hers?"

"She's been leading with negative motivation for a long time, and it's worked," Hannah replied. "She's been fighting me since the day I got here because I believe we can get farther with positive motivation. I took her stick away, and told her she could have it back when she put a carrot on the end of it. She doesn't like the new culture. In fact, her absence from the meeting is just another example of her attempt to maintain control."

"That explains why she's threatened by you, but why is she threatened by me?"

"Carmen is threatened by change," Hannah said. "She sees you as someone young and eager, and is concerned you may embrace my style of leadership."

"I can handle her," Seth responded with complete confidence. "Should I be concerned with any of the others?"

"I'll let you run with your gut feeling about the rest."

"You were analyzing my ability to quickly assess someone's character," Seth stated with a smile. "Was I close?"

"You were very close," Hannah replied. "But don't get too confident. Quite frankly, these three weren't that hard to figure out. Your hardest work assessing character hasn't even begun. Let's talk about your team."

THE CHALLENGE

Hannah explained that the office was broken into four equal teams, and Seth was inheriting the "misfit" team.

"The office is driven by numbers, and the managers compete with each other for bragging rights in each area we measure," Hannah explained. "The team you're inheriting hasn't performed well at all. In fact, they're in last place in each area of measurement."

"Great," Seth replied with sarcasm. "I get the worst of the bunch."

"It's not as bad as it sounds. I plan to mix up the teams and create a new one for you to lead. I don't want you to have the responsibility of leading the worst employees."

Seth thought about her comment for a moment. "Just out of curiosity, how can it be that all the bad employees ended up on the same team?"

"I suppose they've had bad leadership so long they just ended up that way," Hannah answered. "But don't worry. I'll level out the playing field when I mix up the teams."

Seth wondered about Hannah's comment about bad leadership. "Do you think they perform so poorly because of bad leadership, or a lack of leadership?"

"That's an interesting question. I suppose it's a combination of both."

For the next few hours, Hannah explained how the office worked, and put him through the traditional orientation. Over lunch, he learned more about Halifax and the story behind this relatively new call center.

Although a call center already existed in Austin, the company leadership was excited to see rooftops popping up all over this suburb outside Austin. When the decision was made to expand operations by opening a new call center, they chose this area because they believed there would be plenty of potential employees in case others didn't want to transfer from Austin. They were right. About half the office was staffed with call center reps who were willing to transfer, and the other half joined the company two years ago when this new call center opened.

As the day proceeded, Seth was getting more and more excited about the opportunities this job would provide. Although he couldn't soak up the information fast enough, it was time to head back to the airport for his flight home. Sometimes excitement can cause a person to make commitments he or she will later regret.

BRING ON THE MISFITS

In the car on the way back to the airport, Hannah asked, "So what do you think? Are you up to the task of helping me build a culture of employee engagement in this organization?"

"I'm your guy. However, I'm going to ask you to do something for me. You mentioned earlier that you planned to mix up the teams and create a new one for me to lead so I won't have the responsibility of leading the worst employees. Do me a favor. Leave the teams just as they are. I want the challenge of turning this team around."

"Are you sure? You haven't even had the opportunity to meet these people yet."

"I'm absolutely certain," Seth replied. "I just don't believe people show up to work every day and try to make things bad. They certainly didn't start out that way. And if they've become disengaged, maybe someone or something inside the company did it to them. I've shown up to every job I've ever had with the excitement to do great work, and it always seemed to be a boss that took away that excitement. I just think most people want to do good things, and that a good boss can encourage them to do it. I want the challenge of bringing them back to the top."

"And if you're wrong?"

"I don't think I am," Seth replied. "With your commitment to change the culture and my desire to help make it happen, I can do this. But if I'm wrong, I certainly can't do any damage. They're already the poorest performers you have. They can't get any worse!"

As Seth got out of the car at the airport, Hannah looked over and said, "I'll see you in two weeks. Be prepared for the challenge of your life."

Seth thought back on the success he'd had leading in the past, and confidently replied, "I commit to you I'll be ready." He had no idea how hard it would be to keep his commitment.

FIRST DAY

Seth was hoping for a warm reception his first day on the job. It certainly didn't start out that way: No one told him he needed a code to get into the building. It was the first week of January, so he was getting rather cold waiting outside the call center for someone to answer the intercom. Just as he was about to give up and go sit in his car until someone came along, the buzzer sounded and the door unlocked.

Seth walked down a long hallway to the entrance to the call center. The first person he saw when he opened the door was Hannah. "Welcome," she said with a huge smile and warm handshake. "I saw you on the security monitor at the front door, and realized I forgot to give you the code. Sorry about that. We'll get it taken care of today. Let me show you to your cubicle."

As Seth walked through the office, it became apparent that everyone knew it was his first day on the job. The heads started popping up over the cubicle walls the second the door closed behind him.

As Seth put down his box of personal items, Hannah pulled up a chair and sat down. "Here's your first assignment, and you have all day to complete it. I want you to spend the day meeting with each manager one-on-one. Also, schedule a meeting with your entire team to introduce yourself."

"Anything in particular you hope I get from the one-on-one meetings?"

"Nothing specific," she responded. "I just want you to spend some time with them. Get to know them a little, and be prepared to share your observations with me."

"I can do that."

As she walked to the doorway, Hannah suddenly turned around and dropped a report on Seth's desk. "Oh," she said. "I almost forgot. Here's a little challenge I want you to start thinking about. Your team has an attendance problem. As you'll see in this report, of the four teams in the office, yours is in last place. You need to fix this problem."

"How do I fix an attendance problem?"

"I don't know, hotshot," Hannah smiled. "That's for you to figure out. I'll be in meetings all day, so let's schedule some time this evening. There's a small restaurant three blocks from here called La Cantina. We passed it on the way in from the airport when you were here two weeks ago. Meet me there at 6 o'clock. I'll be eager to hear your thoughts."

SOME TIME WITH JILL

Seth was looking forward to spending time with each manager and his team. If there was anything Seth did well, it was build relationships. He planned to call each of his fellow managers to schedule a time to meet, but before he did, he reached over and grabbed the attendance report Hannah had left on his desk. He figured this would be a good topic for discussion in his one-on-ones with the other managers.

Seth started looking through the numbers. He suddenly realized he was being watched. All four manager cubicles were situated along the same wall, and each had a window that looked out into the call center. When he looked up, he saw the call center reps' heads disappear behind the computer stations.

Seth went back to reviewing the report. He figured the best place to start was the worst employee. He looked down at the bottom of the list to find his first target. Her name was Mattie. Seth hoped the other managers could provide some insight in how to deal with his first challenge.

Armed with a great discussion point for his one-on-ones, Seth planned to call each manager to schedule a time to meet. He figured he'd take some time to unpack and get settled in before he made the first call. Just as he reached for his box, Jill walked in.

"Welcome to your first official day in the working world."

"Thank you, Jill. I was going to call you this morning to see if I could schedule some time to meet today. Is now a good time?"

"Now is a great time," Jill replied as she walked over and sat in the chair next to Seth's desk. "I've got a meeting with an employee in a half hour, but I'm free until then. And by the way, you don't need to schedule time with the other managers. Just stop by. It's very informal around here."

"So tell me," Seth asked, "what have I gotten myself into?"

"An overwhelming workload," Jill responded. "We have so much work to do, and now Hannah is here making a bunch of changes. Half of our employees came over from Austin and have many years of service, and half of them are relatively new to Halifax. The new ones are young and open to change, and the older ones want to keep everything the same. With Hannah, you either go along with the change, or she's probably going to make it pretty difficult for you. I guess if you don't mind giving away all your power, then you'll fit in just fine."

"Can I ask you a question about my first challenge?"

"First challenge?" Jill laughed. "You've been here 15 minutes! Hannah sure didn't give you much time to settle in. What's it about?"

"Attendance."

"You have inherited a team with horrible attendance," Jill replied. "I heard you passed up on the opportunity to get a new team. You'll wish you hadn't made that deal. Quite frankly, I'm glad you did though because it means I don't have to take on any of that team. I used to work with some of those people, and there are some bad apples in that group."

"I'm willing to take on the challenge. I'm just not sure how to start."

"If it were me," Jill responded, "I wouldn't rock the boat too much. Anything you do that's drastic will cause problems, and it's just not worth the hassle. Tell them they need to start coming to work, and follow the procedures for discipline if they don't. That's about all you can do. Hannah would probably disagree, but she doesn't seem to be bothered by the conflict."

"The conflict doesn't bother me, either. I just want to see an improvement. What can you tell me about Mattie?"

"Aahh, Mattie," Jill responded. "We worked together in Austin. She didn't have an attendance problem back then. In fact, she had perfect attendance for years. It wasn't until we transferred to this new office and she got a new boss that it became a problem."

"Who was her new boss?"

"Carmen," Jill replied. "When Mattie's attendance became a problem, Carmen ran her off after the first year. She doesn't have much patience for that kind of stuff. The manager you're replacing agreed to take her on her team, but Mattie didn't get any better."

"How could she go from having perfect attendance on one team to being the worst on this team?"

"I don't know," Jill responded. "Probably some personal issues, and you can't get wrapped up with that stuff. If you do, you'll spend all your time in this office."

"I appreciate your thoughts. I need to schedule a meeting with my entire team. How do I do that?"

"Talk to Carmen," Jill replied. "She does all the scheduling, and can get everyone scheduled off the system for a one-hour meeting with you. On most days, you may have only half your team working at the same time. Hannah asked Carmen to schedule your entire team to work today so you could have a team meeting, so they're all here."

For the rest of their time together, Seth did what he did best. He led a conversation focused on Jill's personal life. Seth knew people liked to talk about themselves, and he gave her all the attention she needed.

Jill suddenly looked at her watch and said, "I've got to get ready for my meeting. Good luck with your team meeting." With that, Seth's first one-on-one was over. If only they all would be this easy.

COLD ENCOUNTER

Seth headed to Carmen's office to schedule his team meeting as soon as Jill walked out. He didn't know what to expect after their first encounter two weeks earlier, but he was prepared for anything.

"Good morning," Seth blurted out as he entered Carmen's office.

"What can I do for you, Seth?" Carmen responded without even looking up from her computer screen. Seth wasn't surprised at all that Carmen didn't even bother welcoming him to his new job.

"I need to schedule a meeting with my team for today, and Jill said you were the manager in charge of the schedules."

Carmen continued to stare at her computer while Seth stood in her doorway feeling rather awkward. "Three o'clock this afternoon. You have them for an hour."

"Thanks," Seth replied. "While I'm here, Hannah has asked that I spend some time with each of the managers today. I was wondering if this was a good time to talk."

"Not right now. I'm preparing some information for a meeting. I'll be done by 4:30. Come by then."

Seth thanked her for scheduling the team meeting, and headed back to his office. Just as he got back to his office, Aaron walked out of the cubicle right next to his office.

"There you are," Aaron said. "I was just looking for you. I wanted to see if you'd like to have lunch today."

"I've been in Carmen's office scheduling a team meeting. I was hoping to spend some time with you today, so lunch would be perfect. I'll be ready to leave at noon."

With a few hours to spare, Seth finally found the time to unpack his personal items and get settled in.

SOME TIME WITH AARON

"My first piece of advice is this," Aaron said as they sat down in the crowded diner across the street from the office. "Be nice to the waitresses. It's the only restaurant in walking distance of the office, and you're going to be eating here a lot."

Seth wasn't sure why, but he was very comfortable around Aaron. He got the feeling Aaron was genuine, and that he really enjoyed working for Halifax.

Seth started the conversation. "What do you like best about being a part of the management team?"

"Learning. Hannah has such a great track record of success. I'm not always sure her ideas are the right ones for our office, but I give them a try because she's been so successful. But I admit it's hard. Every time I make a decision about managing my employees, I always think back to how I was managed. But Hannah has been reminding us that these young people have had different life experiences, and it requires us to manage them a little different."

"What do you like least about being a part of the management team?" Seth asked.

"The hours. Before I got promoted, I looked at how management came in at 8 and left at 5. When I got promoted, I assumed I would do the same. And before Hannah arrived, I did. Although sometimes I leave at 5 if my son has a baseball game, I'm normally here much later. My wife doesn't like how much I'm working, but I love the opportunity to learn from Hannah, and my team's results have been improving. We are constantly in the running for first place in just about every area we measure."

After they ordered their lunch, Seth continued his questioning. "Aaron, you seem to enjoy the fact that Hannah has become a part of the team. Do you think the other managers feel the same way?"

"I don't like talking about the other managers. However, I will say this. I sometimes think the changes Hannah has made are more difficult for the others to accept."

"Why do you suppose they have such a difficult time accepting the changes?" Seth asked.

"Two things. One, change often creates more work, and I'm not sure Jill wants additional work. And two, admitting that a new way of doing things may be better is like admitting your old way was wrong, and I'm not sure Carmen wants to admit her way was wrong."

Seth knew his time with Aaron was limited, and he wanted to get his thoughts on Mattie, so he pressed on. "What can you tell me about Mattie?"

"Aahh, Mattie. What a disappointment she's been the past two years. She hasn't always been that way."

Seth pushed for more. "I heard she had perfect attendance years ago, but somehow became disengaged. What do you know about her situation?"

"Mattie was on my team at the old office. She was one of my best employees, ranking toward the top of every area we measured. After we transferred out here and changed the teams, she seemed to go downhill."

"Any idea what caused her to go downhill?" Seth asked.

"It all started when she joined Carmen's team. Carmen manages with an iron fist. She believes management is very simple. Tell people what you expect them to do, and if they don't do it, you beat them until they do."

"Interesting philosophy," Seth laughed. "I've worked for a few people who must have graduated from the same management program. What do you think I should do about Mattie's attendance problem?"

"I don't know," Aaron replied. "It's a tough call. It depends what tone you want to set. If you don't do anything, you could be seen as a pushover, and everyone will assume it is business as usual. If you discipline her, you could be seen as a bully and scare everyone into action. At least they would know you mean business. Whatever you do, good luck."

While they ate their lunch, the conversation turned from business life to personal life. Aaron didn't seem to have any aspirations to take over the world. He simply wanted to be a good father and boss . . . in that order.

TEAM MEETING

Seth hadn't been nervous at any point since his arrival. He wasn't nervous about meeting Hannah on his initial visit, and he wasn't nervous about meeting his fellow managers. But now he was a little nervous. He was about to meet his team.

No one knew the power of first impressions like Seth. He felt he had mastered first impressions over the years, but he wasn't sure how he should come across to his team. If he seemed too confident, they would think he was a "know-it-all." If he seemed too laid back, they would think he wasn't strong enough to lead. He had a plan, and he was about to figure out if it would work.

Seth was in the conference room at 2:45 waiting for everyone to arrive. At 3 o'clock sharp, all twenty-five members of his team filed in like they were attending a funeral. No one spoke, and most stared at the ground. Although there were ten chairs around the conference table, only six people sat down. Everyone else stood along the walls.

Seth got it started. "Good afternoon. My name is Seth Owen, and as you know by now, I am your new manager. We don't have much time, and I want each of you to introduce yourself, so I'm not going to be saying much in this meeting. However, there are two things I want you to know. First, Hannah offered to divide this team to create four new teams in the office because, as a group, you have not performed well. I asked her not to do that."

A few people looked up from the floor as though Seth's words had suddenly piqued their interest.

"Some of you may think I'm crazy for doing that," Seth continued, "particularly since I don't know any of you yet. But I don't need to know you individually to know you all have the potential to be the best in this office. I'm committed to helping make this team the best."

Now all eyes were on Seth.

"Second, many of you in this room have been here a long time. Each of you has forgotten more about your job than I will ever learn. I have no plans to come in here and learn your jobs so I can tell you what you're doing wrong. My plan is to use my position as a manager to remove the road-blocks that keep you from being successful. I'll make you a deal. You do your job well, and I promise you I'll do mine well."

That was it. Seth wanted his team to know two simple things. One, he had confidence in them. And two, he planned to lead them. He would let everything else fall into place from there. After they finished their introductions, Seth realized the people in that room seemed different than the people who walked in an hour earlier. This was a good thing, but sometimes good things don't last.

SOME TIME WITH CARMEN

Seth was so wrapped up in the moment he didn't realize an hour had gone by. Everyone in the room knew it when Carmen came barging in.

"Your hour is up," she said coldly. "Customer hold time is going through the roof because we're short twenty-five people. Everyone back to work."

Seth noticed how the energy was suddenly sucked out of the room when Carmen walked in. The light mood he had created during their introductions was gone in a second. In fact, Seth noticed a change in facial expressions the moment Carmen entered the room.

Not wanting to impact customer hold times, Seth quickly thanked his team and told them he would be following up with one-on-one meetings with each of them. He used the next half hour to make notes regarding each of his team members, then headed to Carmen's office for his 4:30 meeting.

If Seth felt a certain comfort level around Aaron, it was just the opposite with Carmen. Beyond what he had been told about her management style, he just had bad vibes. The fact that she had walked into the conference room and ordered his employees back to work sent a message to Seth about what she thought of him. If he was going to stand a chance, it would require him to stand toe-to-toe with her from the beginning.

"Let's make a deal," Seth said as he walked into Carmen's cubicle without knocking. "You don't bark out orders to my team, and I won't bark out orders to yours."

"Excuse me," Carmen responded as she put down her pen and spun around in her chair to face Seth.

Seth pulled up a chair next to Carmen's desk and said, "You walked into the conference room and instructed my employees to get back to work. I may be new, but I'm pretty certain it's my job to provide them instructions."

"You didn't get them back to work on time, and . . ."

Seth put up his hand and interrupted Carmen before she could finish her comment.

"I understand I should have been watching the clock and gotten them back to work on time," Seth admitted. "I promise you I will improve on that the next time I have a team meeting. However, if there is something you need my employees to do in the future, I would appreciate you bringing it to my attention. I will handle it the way I believe is the most appropriate."

"I'll try to remember that," Carmen responded sarcastically. "But what this team needs is discipline. They've been allowed to get away with anything. They've run the last two managers off, and they need a firm hand to get them in line."

"I appreciate you sharing your observation. You very well may be right about the discipline, and I'll determine that as I get to know them. In the meantime, I plan to build a culture within my team, and part of that culture involves me defending them when someone else tries to give them direction."

"Is there anything specific you want to discuss. I'm leaving at 5."

"Yes, there is," Seth replied. "I've been given the task of improving the attendance of my team, and I'm trying to figure out how I should begin."

"That's easy. Find the worst one and send him packing."

"I have found the worst one," Seth replied, "but it's not a 'him,' it's a 'her.'"

"Who is it?"

"Mattie," Seth replied.

"Aahh, Mattie. She used to be on my team, and she put in for a transfer because she couldn't stand the heat. If you're smart, you'll make an example of her early, and hope it actually makes a difference to the others. You would send a strong message that you won't tolerate lousy performance by firing her now."

"You don't think I should give her a chance to improve?" Seth asked.

"She's had two years to improve. If she hasn't improved by now, she never will. There is nothing that will motivate her. If you want a termination to stick, you'll have to build a case to terminate her."

Seth knew from his conversations with Jill and Aaron that Mattie became disengaged when she joined Carmen's team, so he thought he'd see what she'd be willing to admit.

"I heard Mattie was a pretty good performer when she worked for Aaron, and that she changed when she joined your team. Do you have any idea what caused the change?"

Carmen was not happy with the inference that she had something to do with Mattie's poor performance. "First of all, Aaron is a pushover. He's afraid to tell people when they aren't doing their job. He's more interested in having his team like him, and spends way too much time coddling his employees. In fact, if he spent more time doing his job instead of holding their hands, he'd probably be a better manager."

Despite Carmen's rant about Aaron, Seth calmly replied, "I wasn't asking about Aaron. I was asking if you knew why Mattie's performance changed when she joined your team."

"Because I wasn't willing to pamper her," Carmen shouted.

Seth looked out the cubicle window to the computer stations and noticed everyone close to her office peering over their cubicle walls. Their heads quickly disappeared when they saw Seth look their way, and he knew it was probably time to wrap up this discussion.

Seth had spent time with Jill and Aaron getting to know them personally, but he had no interest in doing that with Carmen. She was cold and calculating, and he didn't want to waste his time. Instead, he decided to change the subject.

"What's it been like since Hannah joined the team?" Seth asked.

"Quite frankly, she's making too many changes. We were successful before she got here, and she seems to be making changes just to make herself look good. She knows everyone from the corporate office is watching her every move, and they expect her to do things differently. If I had been promoted into that job, we would not be making most of these changes."

Throughout the rest of their time together, Carmen made it very clear she didn't care much for Hannah. Now that Seth knew Carmen believed she should have been promoted to Hannah's position, he was beginning to understand Carmen's motives and anger.

In the middle of their conversation, Carmen stood up and began collecting her things. "It's 5 o'clock, and I have to go," she said. "We'll have to finish this conversation another time." She walked out of her office and left Seth sitting alone.

WORK WHENEVER YOU WANT

Seth thought it was strange that someone in management would knock people over trying to get out of the building at 5 o'clock. On his way back to his office, he noticed all the other managers had left, too. Seth looked across the call center and noticed Hannah's light was still on, so he walked to her office. She was gathering her things to leave for the day as Seth walked into her office, so he asked, "What hours am I supposed to work?"

Without looking up she said, "I don't care what hours you work. I'm more interested in your performance than I am in how many hours you work. Work whenever you want."

Seth stood in her doorway in utter disbelief. After a moment of silence he said, "I just assumed I would have to do the typical 8 to 5 routine."

"Seth, I'm going to give you certain tasks, and will expect those tasks to be completed and for you to exceed my expectations. As long as you do that, I don't care if you work four hours a day. Now, if you'll excuse me, I have an errand to run before our meeting. I'll see you at La Cantina at 6 o'clock."

Hannah headed for the door, and Seth headed back to his office. He had some time to kill before he left for La Cantina, so he used the time making additional notes from his team meeting. When he was done, he headed out the door to meet Hannah.

INTRODUCTION TO LA CANTINA

Hannah was not exaggerating when she said the restaurant was small. She was already sitting in the corner when Seth arrived.

"I hope you like margaritas," she said as the waiter placed two margaritas on the table. "They're the best in town."

As Seth sat down, Hannah got straight to the point. "So tell me about your first day."

"Where would you like me to start?"

"Start with your one-on-ones," Hannah said. "What did you think of your fellow managers?"

"I think they each have very different views of managing their teams. They all seem to be confident in their approach, but their methods are certainly different."

"Did you see a method you preferred?" Hannah asked.

"Well, I certainly don't prefer Carmen's approach, and Jill isn't setting the world on fire. If I had to pick someone to follow, it would be Aaron."

"I'm glad to hear that," Hannah responded. "When I was first moved into this position, I noticed the managers here seemed to spend more time managing their teams than leading them. I explained that most employees are sick of being managed, and are starving for leadership. Aaron was the only manager to really make an effort to change. His team has responded well to his approach. In fact, he has the most engaged team in the office."

"How did he do it?"

"Up to this point, it's been based mostly on his personality," Hannah answered. "He is outgoing and cares about his employees, and they've reacted well to his approach. Perhaps the most exciting thing is that creating engaged employees is about much more than personality. It certainly helps to have a little charisma, but the methods needed to create a culture of employee engagement can be learned."

"I want to learn how to do it," Seth responded eagerly. "After an hour with my team today, I saw a spark of hope. I just don't know how to start the process." Seth was eager to learn, and Hannah was eager to teach.

A GLIMPSE AT THE FUTURE

Seth was like a ball of clay, ready to be molded. Hannah knew it and reached across the table and removed a pen from Seth's shirt pocket. She pulled the napkin out from underneath her drink.

"While you were gone the past two weeks, I had an end-of-year meeting with the management team," Hannah said. "I introduced a concept to the team and explained we would spend time this year going deeper with the concept. I'm going to share it with you so you'll be caught up before our first quarterly meeting this month."

Hannah started by drawing a triangle on the napkin. Then she wrote *Engaged Leadership* across the top. "Over the years, I've determined that if we're going to have engaged employees, we must have engaged leadership. Too often we find ourselves blaming the employees for being disengaged, when the real problem is disengaged leadership. We simply don't provide the three aspects of leadership that lead to engagement."

She then drew four puzzle pieces inside the triangle. In the first puzzle piece she wrote the word
Directional.

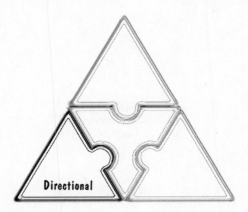

Before Hannah could speak, Seth blurted out,
"That must be about having a vision for the future,
and knowing what direction we're taking."

"That's certainly one aspect of it. But it goes
deeper than that. While managers have a responsibility for setting the vision of their organization,
they have an obligation to build a consensus for
that vision. It's not just a matter of coming up with
the vision and hoping people will see it. It's a
matter of getting buy-in. It's what I refer to as
Directional Leadership."

"How will you ever get everyone in the organization to agree with the vision?"

"We don't have to get everyone to agree *with* the
vision," Hannah replied. "We just have to get
everyone to agree *to* the vision. There are many
aspects of Directional Leadership, and I plan to
share these responsibilities with you and the other
managers in our manager meetings. It will become
clearer as we build the model."

"What's the second aspect of Engaged Leadership?"

In the second puzzle piece, Hannah wrote the word *Motivational*.

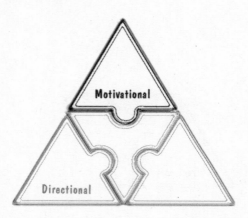

"As you build consensus for the vision using Directional Leadership, you have a responsibility to inspire employees to want to pursue that vision," Hannah explained. "It's not enough to build consensus for the vision if you don't inspire people to want to pursue it. It's what I refer to as *Motivational Leadership*," Hannah explained.

"Don't employees have a responsibility to show up with their own inspiration? After all, they are paid to do their job."

"True," Hannah replied, "but as we've discussed, most employees are disengaged. They show up and do the minimum to get by so they can collect a paycheck. The first step toward engaging employees is to let them feel they are part of a bigger picture, and we do that in Directional Leadership. But if we truly want to build an organization with engaged employees, we must make sincere efforts to recognize and inspire them."

"Fair enough. What's the third aspect of Engaged Leadership?"

In the third puzzle piece, Hannah wrote the word *Organizational.*

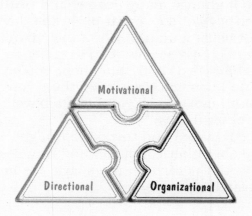

Seth sat quietly this time and waited for Hannah's explanation.

"This third aspect is about developing the team to realize the vision. It doesn't matter if you've walked hand-in-hand with your team to build consensus for the future and put in place wonderful ways to inspire those team members if you haven't developed the team to realize the vision. It's the third aspect of Engaged Leadership, and it's what I refer to as *Organizational Leadership.*"

Hannah then put the cap back on the pen and leaned across the table to place it back in Seth's shirt pocket. She didn't say a word.

"I give up," Seth said smiling. "What's the center piece of the puzzle?"

"That can wait for one of our quarterly meetings. The first one is tomorrow."

After Hannah paid the bill and they were getting ready to leave, she said, "You know, you remind me of myself when I started working at Halifax. All the energy in the world and innocent enough to think you can do it. Over time, that will change. I encourage you to not let it change you. I've seen it change many people, and I believe it's because they got so caught up in the day-to-day aspect of being a manager that they didn't spend any time being a leader. You're going to have a responsibility to do both, but I hope you never lose the spark. I can teach you everything you need to know, but I can't teach you how to have a spark. Don't ever let that go."

As Seth tossed and turned that night, he kept thinking about her comment, and promised himself he would never lose the spark. He hoped he could keep his promise.

THE FIRST-QUARTER MEETING

Seth was single, and he liked it that way. He didn't want a marriage and kids to get in the way of his professional career. He had seen too many friends get married early, and some were already divorced. He wanted to wait for his career to get off the ground. There would be plenty of time for marriage later in life.

Aside from the professional reasons Seth wasn't getting married anytime soon, he really liked the flexibility that came with being single. Seth was not a morning person, so he was more than thrilled with Hannah's position on work hours. Since he wouldn't be very productive the first couple hours of the day, he decided it would make more sense if he went in to work a little later.

But today was management meeting day. In return for her flexibility, Hannah required all managers to be in the conference room at 8 AM sharp on meeting days. Seth wanted to make a good impression, so he got there early. As he walked into the conference room at 7:45, everyone but Hannah was already there. So much for making a good impression.

"Am I late?" Seth asked.

"Not at all," Aaron replied. "We just aren't late to this management meeting. Hannah made it clear on her first day that anyone who walked into this meeting late would have to wash her car in the company parking lot."

"Has anyone ever been late?" Seth asked.

Everyone turned to Jill and smiled.

"I'm late to everything," Jill replied. "But after that public humiliation the first month, I'm the first one here every meeting."

Aaron continued to tease Jill about the car wash as Hannah walked in and closed the door behind her.

"Great," she said. "Everyone is here. Let's get started."

Carmen stood up to pass out the monthly reports when Hannah put up her hand. "Carmen, we won't need the monthly reports today. We're going to do something a little different."

Hannah's words got everyone's attention. "As you know, every January the corporate office sends out adjustments to the annual strategic plan. The good news is there aren't any major changes to the plan. However, there are some adjustments that will affect you and your teams. We'll spend the first part of the morning reviewing those changes."

As Hannah sat down, Carmen rolled her eyes. "Great, more work from the Ivory Tower. They must have gotten word we don't have enough work to do already."

Hannah ignored Carmen's remark and passed out a document that appeared to be nearly an inch thick. "I just got off an early morning conference call with my peers from the other call centers, and there appears to be only two changes that will have a direct impact on the management team. First, by the end of the month we will be required to perform an Employee Engagement Survey."

Jill jumped in immediately. "I think you mean an Employee Satisfaction Survey. I organized a survey for the office when I first got promoted, and I'm sure I've got a copy of it in my office. I'll go find it so we can get it out as soon as possible."

As she stood up, Hannah interrupted her. "There's no need for that. The company is using an outside firm to conduct the survey. And yes, I meant an Employee Engagement Survey."

Carmen spoke up. "First of all, what in the world is an Employee Engagement Survey? And why are they wasting the company's money on that? I'm sure whatever it is we can do internally for a lot less money."

"I'll answer your second question first," Hannah replied. "They want honest feedback on the survey, and we have a better chance of getting it if our employees don't fear retribution from an internal survey. And besides, the results of the survey tie directly to the second change, which I'll explain in a minute."

Carmen responded in an exasperated tone of voice, "Great. More good news I'm sure."

"Now," Hannah continued, "I'll answer your first question. An Employee Engagement Survey is designed to measure an employee's engagement, not his or her satisfaction. I'm sure we have plenty of employees who are perfectly satisfied being disengaged, so an Employee Satisfaction Survey won't reveal anything about how well we are leading our employees toward engagement."

"Why are they concerned with this employee engagement thing?" Jill asked. "Last year we were told we needed to retain employees, now we're being told we need to engage them. Why are we changing?"

"First of all, disengaged employees are costing companies billions of dollars a year," Hannah stated, "and they want to see how well we've created a culture of employee engagement. And second, if our goal is employee retention instead of engagement, then we'll probably spend an enormous amount of time retaining disengaged employees."

"Who is 'they'?" Carmen asked.

"The corporate office," Hannah replied.

"Is this really coming from the corporate office, or is this just something you're making us do?" Carmen asked.

"Every call center in the company is required to conduct an Employee Engagement Survey," Hannah answered. "To be honest, I'm as surprised as you are about the whole thing. But I've been telling you about the importance of employee engagement since I got this job, and now the company is ensuring that we're all doing our part."

"What an enormous waste of time!" Carmen grumbled. "My team results are just fine. What difference does it make what this Employee Engagement Survey says about me?"

"It will mean a lot to you when I explain the second change," Hannah said. "The survey will be conducted this month, and a follow-up survey will be done in December. Our end-of-year bonus this year will depend on how much improvement is made when they conduct the survey again in December."

When the managers in the room heard that part of their compensation would be tied to their ability to engage employees, the room was hushed. No one said a word, until Jill broke the silence.

"I think it's a great idea. I'm not afraid of what my employees have to say about the way I manage them."

"Of course you don't," Carmen responded. "You let your employees do whatever they want. Half of them are your old friends. I'm sure you'll get glowing remarks from your team."

Aaron finally spoke up. "Carmen, you're just afraid the survey will reveal the cruel and unusual punishment techniques you use. Do you still have the torture chamber in your office?"

Carmen didn't find the humor in his comment. "Shut up, Aaron. Just because I'm the only manager in the office who will tell these people like it is doesn't mean my techniques are cruel and unusual."

"I'm just kidding, Carmen! I agree with Jill. I think it's a great idea, and I'm looking forward to it. Besides, if we're doing the right things to build a culture of employee engagement, then we shouldn't fear what our employees have to say on this survey. And if our employees truly are engaged, then we'll make our bonuses at the end of the year."

Seth had been quiet the entire meeting. While some of the others spoke, he was flipping through the rest of the strategic plan Hannah had passed out at the beginning of the meeting. Hannah looked over at him and asked, "Seth, what do you think?"

"Well, I'm certainly not afraid of what they'll say on the survey this month since it won't be my

leadership ability they're assessing. I'm more concerned with what they say on the one in December.
After looking through this document, it seems the
entire year could be spent just managing the tasks
associated with the strategic plan. The challenge
will be finding time to develop our employees."

"Now you know why some of us are concerned
about all this engagement stuff," Carmen replied.

"Us?" Aaron asked with a smile on his face. "By
my count, you are the only one who's voiced any
concern." Aaron seemed to get a great deal of joy
from his jabs at Carmen.

Carmen didn't bother replying to Aaron's comment. Hannah looked up and said, "We won't have
much control over what the survey says about us
this month, so there's no need to worry about it.
However, we can control what the survey says about
us at the end of the year if we focus on building a
culture of employee engagement. I've done it in
every organization I've been a part of, and I know
I can do it with this one. If you're willing to learn, I'm
willing to coach each of you through the process."

"I'm in," Jill and Aaron said in unison. Hannah
looked at Seth, who nodded in agreement. Carmen
looked up and said, "Sure, whatever, but I'm going
to need more coffee for this."

54 PERCENT

As the management team returned from a short
break, Seth noticed Hannah had set up two flipcharts at the front of the room. On one she had
written *54 Percent*. As everyone took their seats,
Hannah walked over and underlined it before sitting down.

"At our end-of-year meeting a couple weeks ago,
I shared with you a leadership model I refer to as

Engaged Leadership," she started. "I spent some time with Seth yesterday explaining the model to him, so you all have the same information. Now, if we're going to have any success at all creating a culture of employee engagement, it's important for us to know how Engaged Leadership works. But before we look at the first aspect of the model, I want to discuss what I've written on the flipchart."

"That's the percentage of bonus Carmen will receive at the end of the year," Aaron laughed.

Carmen shot daggers with her eyes toward Aaron and was about to respond when Hannah jumped in, "It could be if we don't understand the real meaning of it." She finally got Carmen's attention. In fact, she got everyone's attention.

"The Gallup Organization did research on employee disengagement years ago and found 54 percent of employees are disengaged," Hannah explained. "The good news is the study showed 29 percent are engaged, and the bad news is the remaining 17 percent are actively disengaged."

"I seem to be spending more and more of my time with the actively disengaged," Jill said.

"You're not alone," Hannah replied. "Most managers do, and I'd be willing to bet most of the managers in the other call centers will be spending their time with the actively disengaged. We'll certainly deal with our actively disengaged employees, and we'll be learning how to do that. We'll also learn how to deal with our 29 percent at the top of the organization."

"I don't worry about those people," Carmen interrupted. "They are the only ones I can depend on. I just give them a task and get out of the way. The last thing they want is to hear from me."

"That's a mistake many leaders make," Hannah said. "Unfortunately, when we leave the top

29 percent alone, they tend to be the first to leave. We'll be discussing how to make sure they don't want to leave. In the meantime, I believe our best chance of building employee engagement is by focusing on the 54 percent in the middle."

"If they're disengaged, why should we spend our time with them?" Jill asked. "Maybe we should just focus on the ones producing the work."

"Two reasons, Jill," Hannah replied. "One, the 54 percent in the middle will be assessing you on the Employee Engagement Survey, and will have a negative effect on your bonus if you don't find a way to engage them. And two, . . ."

Jill interrupted Hannah before she could finish. "I don't even need to hear the second reason. Reason number one is good enough for me."

"Then for the benefit of everyone else," Hannah continued, "I'll give the second reason. Employees want to be engaged, and we have a responsibility to them and the company to engage them."

"Fair enough," Aaron said. "How do we get started?"

"This year is going to be a learning year for each of us," Hannah answered. "In addition to our regularly scheduled monthly meetings, we will have a quarterly meeting for the sole purpose of learning Engaged Leadership. This is our first quarterly meeting. We will reschedule our monthly meeting for tomorrow."

"Hannah," Carmen responded, "we already have way too many meetings to attend. Can't we just talk about this stuff at our monthly meetings?"

"No, we can't," Hannah replied. "Our monthly meetings are about updating each other on the state of the business, and I intend for those to continue that way. Learning about Engaged

Leadership may be the most important thing we do all year, and we'll dedicate one morning a quarter to do nothing but learn and share how we applied the concepts in the workplace. I promise you we'll end these meetings by noon."

"I think it's a great idea," Aaron said. "If Hannah has implemented this approach in other offices and it worked, then I'm willing to dedicate one morning a quarter to learning it, particularly if part of my compensation is tied to building a culture of employee engagement. And who knows, maybe we can create a little competition with our old office."

With the exception of Carmen, everyone around the table nodded in agreement.

"As you will recall, there are three aspects of Engaged Leadership," Hannah started. "Now, you can't tackle all of Engaged Leadership at one time, so here's my plan. There are twelve lessons I plan to share with you. This quarter we'll learn the four lessons needed to be good Directional leaders. We'll have the entire quarter to apply what we've learned. In the second quarter, we'll learn the four lessons needed to be good Motivational leaders. Again, we'll have the entire quarter to apply what we've learned. Then in the third quarter, we'll learn the four lessons needed to be good Organizational Leaders. At that point, you will have the complete picture, and will have the next six months to continue making progress toward building a culture of employee engagement."

"What about the fourth quarter?" Aaron asked.

"We'll see how we progress," Hannah said. "Any questions?"

Seth could tell Carmen had something to say, but she managed to stay quiet. It wouldn't last long.

LET THE LEARNING BEGIN

Hannah walked to the second flipchart. She drew a large triangle, and wrote *Engaged Leadership* at the top. Seth knew where Hannah was going with the model when she drew four puzzle pieces inside the triangle. In the first puzzle piece, she wrote the word *Directional*.

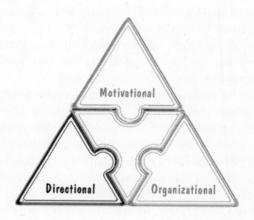

As she sat back down, Hannah said, "As a review, the first aspect is Directional Leadership. For the most part, the direction for this organization has been set by the corporate office. While we may not all agree with every aspect of the vision, we have a responsibility to carry it out."

"I read through some of the changes to the strategic plan during the break," Jill said, "and some of our long-term employees are going to struggle with a few of them. This push to improve how fast we handle calls instead of how well we handle them is not going to go over well with our more senior employees."

"That's expected," Hannah replied. "Our responsibility as leaders is to build a consensus for the vision. We can't just hope our employees will see it and agree to it. We have to get buy-in."

"That will be easier said than done with a few employees," Aaron said.

"I agree," Hannah replied. "There will be some who will never agree to the vision. In fact, there are some employees who have never agreed to the vision, and have done everything they can to disrupt the organization. Those are our 17 percent of actively disengaged employees."

Seth spoke up. "According to everything I've heard so far, a lot more than 17 percent of my employees are actively disengaged."

"That certainly may be the case since your team didn't get much leadership in the past," Hannah replied. "But regardless of where our employees fall today, we have a responsibility to provide Directional Leadership. I'm going to share with you the four lessons related to Directional Leadership."

She walked back to the flipchart and wrote:

1. Recruit support from the Top 29 percent.

She sat back down and said, "This group is critical to our success as an organization. Beyond the fact they normally carry a significant amount of the workload, the top 29 percent have significant influence over the 54 percent in the middle. You see, if we as leaders don't do a good job engaging the 54 percent in the middle, they will look for direction from their peers. They are going to get direction from one of two places. The top 29 percent, or the bottom 17 percent who are actively trying to tear down the organization. Which would you prefer for your team?"

"What if we don't have buy-in from the top 29 percent?" Aaron asked.

"First of all, you can't assume you'll have buy-in. Your first job is to convince them the vision is right. The one thing I know for certain is that if you can't sell the vision to the top 29 percent, then you don't have a chance of selling it to the disengaged employees in the middle."

There was complete silence in the room for a few moments while the lesson began to sink in to everyone around the table. Carmen was the first to break the silence.

"Are you telling me I have to spend my time recruiting supporters to get these people in the middle to do what they're paid to do? Isn't my job to use my influence as their manager to get them to work?"

Aaron jumped in. "Let's face it, Carmen. Your influence is to tell them what to do, and they do it because they know you'll punish them if they don't. I don't mean to be critical, but we all know that's how you influence your employees."

"That's what a manager is supposed to do, Aaron," Carmen replied.

Hannah responded, "Some managers believe that's the way to manage. But what I'm talking about is leadership. This approach is going to require a change in thinking for some of the people around this table."

After another moment of silence, Jill pressed on. "Okay, so we use the influence of our top 29 percent to build consensus with the 54 percent in the middle. What's the next point?"

Hannah returned to the flipchart and wrote:

2. Prepare the organization for change.

She sat back down and said, "It's no surprise that people don't like change. Just look around this table and you'll see some of your peers who aren't comfortable with what I've said so far, and I've only shared one point with you. Remember, your disengaged employees are not bad people. Many of them are doing their jobs. They simply dislike change as much as anyone. Any change will probably put them out of their comfort zone."

"We're all going through change," Carmen groaned.

"Yes, we are," Hannah replied, "but if we just cram the changes down their throat, we'll never build consensus."

Seth asked, "So how do we prepare them for change?"

"For starters, we walk out of this room on the same page," Hannah replied. "Whether you agree with the changes is not the issue. We must be united as a team."

"Okay," Jill said, "we start preparing our teams for change by being united as a management team. What's the next point?"

Jill was doing a good job of moving the discussion forward, but Seth had something else in mind.

"We've been going for a while now. Can we take a break?"

Everyone in the room nodded enthusiastically.

"Ten minutes," Hannah declared. "If you're not all back, I'm starting without you."

BACK TO WORK

Once the managers were all back in their seats, Hannah returned to the flipchart and wrote:

3. Let them know how they contribute.

"This may seem simple," she said, "but all too often we assume our employees know what we want. We can't begin to build a consensus for the vision if we don't communicate our expectations."

"I think we all learned that in Management 101," Carmen said sarcastically. "If someone's not communicating expectations, then they probably shouldn't be in management."

"Some of you are very good at communicating expectations," Hannah replied, "but there is something even more important than communicating the expectation. Can anyone tell me what it is?"

Jill was the first to respond. "I'll take a guess. We have to know how we're going to discipline them if they don't meet the expectation."

"You're close, Jill," Hannah replied. "We have to communicate a consequence. Keep in mind that consequences are not always bad, so it's not always about discipline."

"I think employees know if they don't do what they're told, there's going to be a negative consequence," Carmen responded.

"Perhaps that was taught in your Management 101 class," Hannah replied calmly, "but leaders are taught the power of positive consequences in Leadership 101."

Seth got the impression Hannah was getting annoyed with Carmen's insistence on challenging everything she said. Carmen's silence indicated she might have gotten the same impression.

"Different situations require different consequences," Hannah continued, "and I'll leave that up to you to decide. Just know that a consequence is one of the most important tools we have to change behavior. If we're going to build a consensus, we must ensure employees know what is expected of them, and communicate clear consequences. Any questions?"

No one raised a hand, so Hannah got up and walked back to the flipchart. This time she wrote:

After she sat back down, she said, "We seem to do a good job of informing our employees of changes to our strategic plan, but I'm not sure we do a very good job keeping it in front of them. We must find ways to constantly communicate our progress."

"We had those cards with the vision statement printed and laminated when the strategic plan first came out," Jill said. "We can get those done again."

"Those cards are fine," Hannah said, "but I'm talking about more than just reminding them what the vision statement is. I'm talking about letting them know how we're doing in pursuit of the vision. There are many creative ways to do it. We just need to find some ways to constantly communicate our progress. An uninformed employee is a disengaged employee."

Hannah let her words soak in for a moment. "You now have the four lessons of Directional Leadership. Are there any questions?"

Jill chimed in. "The four lessons are good, but they're somewhat broad. Can you give us some specific examples of how we go about doing each of them?"

"That's a fair observation," Hannah responded. "Part of being a leader is determining what works best for you. If I provide you all the answers, you won't think like a leader. So here's what I want you to do. Over the next quarter, as you work to build a consensus for the vision, I want you to find ways to recruit support from your top 29 percent, and prepare your team for change. I want you to be extremely clear about what you want from your team members, and constantly communicate their progress. At our next quarterly meeting, I'm going to ask you to share what you did in each of these areas."

Hannah looked up at the clock and noticed it was 12 o'clock. "I promised you we would end these meetings by noon, and I'll keep my promise. But I'll leave you with this thought. Your success with Engaged Leadership will depend less on what you know, and more on what you do. I encourage you to take what we've discussed today about Directional Leadership and put it to work. It will be the key to building a culture of employee engagement."

With that, everyone grabbed their things and left the conference room. On his way back to his office, Seth figured if this leadership thing didn't get any harder than this, turning his team around would be simple. Time would tell.

REALITY SETS IN

Seth couldn't believe a month had passed since the first-quarter meeting. Although he intended to create a plan to develop his team, he didn't realize it would take every bit of four weeks just to get settled into his new job. There were procedures to learn, reports to complete, and meetings to attend.

Seth soon realized it took an entire eight-hour day just to manage his daily management tasks.

Despite the workload and the two weeks he was out of the office for training, Seth was determined to schedule one-on-ones with all his team members. While the other managers had the luxury of recruiting support from their top 29 percent when they walked out of the last quarterly meeting, Seth had to spend time with his team members just to determine his top 29 percent. It took him nearly two weeks to get to them all.

"Congratulations," Hannah said as she walked into his office. "The January report just came out, and it shows your team absence percentage improved. You're still in last place, but your overall numbers improved."

"You're kidding."

"No, I'm not," Hannah replied. "I'm anxious to hear what you've been doing. We haven't even gotten to Motivational Leadership, and it seems you're already motivating your team."

"To be honest, I think at this point it's just pure luck. I've been so busy getting into my management routine that I haven't had a chance to spend much time with my team members. I finished my one-on-one meetings, and have identified who I think make up my top 29 percent. Now that I'm getting into somewhat of a routine, I've committed myself to spending more time working with them."

"Like I said, your team's improvement wasn't drastic, but it was something," Hannah remarked. "If you haven't been spending much time with your team, the improvement can probably be attributed to the honeymoon period. Most employees try to impress their new boss because they don't know what to expect if they don't do well. They work a little harder until they know what they can get away with. But I have to say, I've noticed you walk around and greet each employee every morning when you get into the office. They've been starved for that attention, and I'll bet some of the improvement is directly related to your efforts. Keep up the good work."

After Hannah left, Seth felt a little guilty that he hadn't done more to impact the improvement of his team. He knew the honeymoon period would be over soon, and that his team would give up on him if he didn't start making some things happen.

GOING FOR THE TOP 29 PERCENT

One of the most pressing issues Seth needed to address was a change in the strategic plan. A key efficiency measurement for each team was Representative Occupancy. Seth discovered this was a fancy term used to describe the amount of time a call center rep actually handled customer calls, as opposed to nonproductive time like meetings and training. Because personnel accounted for nearly two-thirds of the call center's expenses, Hannah wanted to make sure the employees were as productive as possible.

Along with new technology came the opportunity to ensure less idle time for the call center reps. The same procedure for measuring efficiency had been followed for years, and since it was changing, Seth needed to cover the new procedure with his team.

At lunch the day before, Jill informed the other managers she had shared the changes with her team, and she thought she was going to have a mutiny on her hands. Based on the response from Jill's team, Seth anticipated some of his employees would have a problem with the new plan.

He figured this would be a good opportunity to build consensus by recruiting support from his top 29 percent.

He searched through the paperwork on his desk and found the list he had made of employees he considered to be in his top 29 percent. He had circled the names of the six that seemed to be the most engaged in his one-on-one meetings. Fortunately, they were all scheduled to work that day.

Carmen, on the other hand, took the day off. Jill was her backup for the day coordinating the schedules. Although he wasn't intimidated by Carmen, he just didn't like being around her. He was glad it was Jill he had to deal with to get his employees scheduled off for a meeting.

"Jill, I need your help. I have six people I need to meet with this afternoon. Can you schedule a half-hour meeting around 2 o'clock?"

Jill stared at her computer for a moment. "Let's see . . . 2 o'clock doesn't look good because we have some employees scheduled for a late lunch and that will throw off our service levels. How about 3 o'clock?"

"Perfect. Thanks for your help."

Seth didn't mind the extra hour because he knew he'd need it to prepare for the meeting. As he was getting settled into the conference room, his six employees walked in. Seth asked them to take a seat on either side of the table. Although this smaller group was much more outgoing than his entire team on his first day on the job, Seth could sense some confusion from this group. No one knew why he or she was there.

"I've asked to meet with you because I need your help," he started. "After meeting with the entire team in the one-on-one meetings, I consider you to be the best and brightest on the team."

A look of relief could be seen on every face in the room.

"Not only are you the top performers, but you seem to be a group I can confide in. A change has been made in the strategic plan of the organization, and I wanted to run it past you before I shared it with the entire team. The change affects how we measure Representative Occupancy."

After providing a detailed explanation of the change, Seth asked, "Can any of you think of a reason why this would not be good for the team?"

A few team members expressed some concern, and Seth provided reasonable responses to each comment. "Can I count on you for your support of the change?" All the heads around the table nodded in support.

"Good. I anticipate we may have some on our team who won't agree with the change. Any help you can provide supporting the change will be greatly appreciated."

With that, Seth thanked them for their time, and sent them back to work. He felt good about the meeting, and was glad he finally had at least one experience to share at the next quarterly meeting. He headed back to his office and found a note in his chair that read, "Meet me at La Cantina at 6:00—H."

PRIVATE COACHING

Seth felt he was fitting in pretty well with the management team, even though he'd been there just over a month. He still had a lot to learn, but he knew he was making progress. He remembered how excited he was when Hannah told him he could work whenever he wanted. He created in his mind a perfect scenario in which he got to sleep in, get to the office around 9, and stay until the work was done. At this point, he was at the office every morning by 7:30, and the work never got finished.

If there was anything that surprised him, it was the number of managerial tasks that had to be done every day. He didn't think any of it was particularly difficult, just time consuming. When the other managers would complain they didn't have time to spend with their employees, he thought it was just an excuse to avoid dealing with all the people issues. He found the biggest thrill he got from the job was spending time with his employees. He also found the biggest challenge was finding the time to do that.

He appreciated the effort Hannah was making to teach her managers how to build a culture of employee engagement. Seth and some of his old college friends had recently gotten together for a long weekend, and they spent time comparing their job experiences. Seth told them about Hannah, and how she was dedicating time each quarter to develop their leadership skills. None of them had a similar story to tell, but they all had a peer like Carmen.

Although Seth looked forward to the ongoing development he would get in the quarterly meetings and the training he would attend at least once a quarter, he particularly liked the one-on-one time with Hannah at La Cantina. They had only met a few times, but it was like having a personal coach to help him along. He wondered if he was the only manager getting the extra attention, or if everyone enjoyed these private sessions. He got his answer when he arrived at La Cantina.

As he opened the door to the restaurant, Aaron walked out.

"What are you doing here?" Seth asked.

"I just got through spending some time with Hannah. She mentioned you were meeting her at 6. I would stay, but I've got to take my oldest daughter to cheerleading practice. Have a good meeting, and I'll see you in the morning."

Seth walked in and saw Hannah sitting at the same table as before. He figured that must be her office away from the office.

"Where's my margarita?" Seth joked as he sat down.

"No margarita for me today. I have a conference call with my boss at 6:30. He's on a plane right now and can't get to a phone until then. My husband's meeting me here at 7, so you'll get to meet him if you're still here."

"You may have a conference call with your boss at 6:30, but I don't," he laughed. "Where's the waitress?"

After Seth ordered his margarita, Hannah said, "I want to talk to you about your team's attendance problem. Even though your results have improved, you indicated you haven't done much with your team since you've been settling into your new job. Have you given much thought to a specific plan?"

Seth had given a lot of thought to how he should deal with his attendance problem, and could certainly use some advice. "I had hoped to already have a plan in place considering you asked me about it over a month ago. I feel I've let you down since I haven't taken steps to fix the problem."

"You've been busy, I know. Tell me what you would have done if you didn't have to spend a month getting acclimated to your new job."

"Well, I asked the other managers what they thought, and there wasn't any consensus at all. Carmen thought I should fire the worst performer and send a message to the others, and Jill thought I shouldn't rock the boat."

"What did Aaron think?"

"Aaron wasn't much help either," Seth laughed. "He just pointed out the pros and cons of any action I took, and wished me luck."

"What do you think is the right answer?"

"I think the easiest thing to do would be to fire the worst performer," Seth answered. "The problem would be gone, and everyone else on the team would know I'm prepared to take action if they don't perform well."

"Have you met with this person to share your concern about her poor attendance?"

"I have," Seth answered. "I told her she needed to improve. I was extremely clear about what I wanted."

"Did you tell her that if she doesn't, the consequence will be termination?"

"No, I didn't," Seth responded. "I think she walked away knowing I was serious."

"Did you not listen to anything I said at our first quarterly meeting? Did you have your conversation with her before or after the quarterly meeting where we talked about expectations and consequences?"

"After," Seth responded as he stared at the table.

"Then you had the information you needed. The lessons I'm teaching you have no value whatsoever if you don't put them to use. Now, if you want her to be an engaged member of your team, you must provide expectations and consequences. When you do, you give her the power to determine her own fate."

"Do you think the consequence should be termination?" Seth asked.

"I think the consequence has to motivate the behavior you want. If she doesn't need or want this job, then termination will not motivate her to come to work."

"So what consequence should I use?" Seth asked.

"You ask too many questions!" Hannah laughed. "That's a question you're going to have to answer on your own."

Besides getting settled into a new job, Seth was getting settled into a new apartment. He didn't know many people in town, although he had made a few friends at the church he started attending around the corner from his apartment. Other than some guidance from them, Seth was learning his way around on his own. Hannah knew that and spent some time talking about the area. Seth thought maybe she was tired of talking business after a full day and was looking for some lighter conversation.

Hannah looked down at her watch and realized it was almost 6:30. "I have to call my boss," she said. "You can hang out if you want. You've hardly touched your margarita, and I'd love for you to meet my husband."

"No, I need to get home. I'll see you in the morning."

Seth spent most of that night thinking about his attendance issue, and how disappointed he was in himself for letting Hannah down. What he thought should be easy had turned out to be the most difficult, and important, part of his job.

MAKE WAY FOR CHANGE

When Seth initially selected his top 29 percent and scheduled the meeting to recruit support for the change in the Representative Occupancy procedure, he did it so he could show he had made some progress. Quite frankly, he didn't give much thought to the outcome of the meeting.

Seth was out of the office for a few days training, but when he returned he scheduled a meeting with his entire team to announce the change to Representative Occupancy. He wasn't looking forward to the meeting because he knew he would be fighting an uphill battle. In a meeting with Jill the day before, she explained that two of Seth's team members had been instrumental in writing the current procedure, and they would likely defend the status quo.

After Seth explained the change to the group, a few of his team members started squirming in their chairs. The two people Jill warned him would be against the change jumped up and started complaining, and he could see the beginnings of a mutiny. And then something pretty amazing happened. Miles Freeman, one of his top 29 percent, took over.

"Before you go any further," Miles said, "I want to say I think this is a good change." He continued by laying out exactly what he liked about the change, and by the time he was done, most of the other top 29 percent had supported the idea as well. Before long, many of the disengaged employees were agreeing with the change.

Seth realized he didn't need to say a word. He was certain the bottom 17 percent still disagreed, but they were silenced by the agreement in the room. His effort at recruiting support from the top 29 percent had paid off.

After a few moments of silence, Seth pointed to the two employees who had complained about the change. "Please stand up," he instructed. Each had a panicked look on his face.

"Seriously," Seth repeated, "please stand up."

They looked at each other and slowly got out of their chairs. The room was silent as everyone awaited the worst.

"I've asked them to stand because I want you all to get a good look at them. These are the men who were instrumental in writing the current procedure. It has worked well for the past two years and was the foundation of the new procedure. As we begin to make the transition, I want to recognize and thank them for their contributions. They were leaders then, and I anticipate they'll be contributing to new ways of doing things in the future. I think they deserve a round of applause."

Seth wasn't sure if the smiles on their faces were relief from not getting scolded or true appreciation for being recognized, but they both seemed to enjoy the moment as they accepted a round of applause from their peers.

After the meeting was over and everyone had returned to work, Seth walked to Hannah's office to share his experience. He stuck his head in the door and noticed she was on the telephone. She looked up and noticed it was Seth, and motioned for him to wait. When she hung up, he walked in and sat down.

"What's up?"

"I just had an interesting experience," Seth said with a smile, "and I thought I would share it with you." He explained in detail what had happened in his team meeting, and waited for her response.

"Three spectacular things happened in that meeting," Hannah said. "One, you proved that recruiting your top 29 percent can work. Two, you helped the rest of the team deal with change by recognizing and celebrating the old way of doing things. And three, you showed them they don't just work for a manager, they work for a leader."

Seth needed that reinforcement. He felt he had let Hannah down when he hadn't communicated a consequence to Mattie for her poor attendance, and he needed a way to prove he had been paying attention to what she was teaching. This type of reinforcement was what he needed, and it didn't cost the company a dime.

EARLY MORNING SURPRISE

Throughout most of the month of February, Seth was showing up to the office at 7:30 not because he was anxious to get to work. He got there early just so he would have enough time in the day to get all his work done and spend time working with his team.

A college buddy had gotten married over the weekend, and Seth was a groomsman. After a long weekend with friends, he knew his confidence had been renewed when he walked into the office at 6 AM Monday. He was determined to make this the day he dealt with Mattie, and he wanted to get an early start. He also had something else on his mind.

It was March now, and the February reports were available. Seth's improvements had been marginal in January, leaving him in fourth place. He had gotten into a routine in February, which freed up more time to spend with his team. He had shown some leadership throughout the month, and he felt his team was responding. While it was nice to have the feeling, he needed proof to show Hannah and the other managers. He hoped the proof he needed was in the monthly report.

Part of the training he received in January was report production, so he knew how to access the reports. After he sat down, he pulled out his training notes so he could get it right the first time. Just as he began to log in to his computer, Hannah walked into his office.

"What in the world are you doing here at 6 in the morning?" Hannah laughed. "I thought you were in a wedding over the weekend. I didn't expect to see you before noon!"

"It was a long weekend," Seth chuckled, "but I was anxious to see my February attendance report. I couldn't sleep, so I figured I'd come on into the office."

"Do you want to log in and pull your own report," Hannah asked, "or would you like to take a look at my copy? I haven't printed all the reports, but I have the attendance report for the entire office right here in my hand." She set her copy of the report on Seth's desk.

"It looks like someone else was anxious to see the monthly report," Seth laughed as he reached across the desk.

He recognized the report from last month and knew the last page ranked all four managers. He flipped straight to the last page, and found what he'd hoped to find. Seth Owen, a young man with only two months in the real working world, had led his team to third place. After two years of being the worst, they now were out of the basement.

A TIME TO CELEBRATE

Seth was a competitive person, and had grown accustomed to winning just about any competition he entered. At any other time in his life, finishing third in a four-person race would have been devastating. But on this day and in this race, finishing third was like winning a gold medal in the Olympics.

Seth jumped up from his desk and started dancing in the middle of his cubicle. It was a good thing there weren't any employees around yet. If he was trying to show Hannah he couldn't dance, it was working. Seth wasn't sure if she was laughing at his reaction to the news, or if she was genuinely happy for him. He hoped it was both.

He started to give Hannah a hug, and then backed off. He had been through sexual harassment training in January and didn't want to cross a line. Hannah figured that's why he backed off, and extended her arms anyway. "You big dummy," she said with a smile, "give me a hug!"

Seth threw his arms around her to celebrate the moment, but also as a way of thanking her for the support and encouragement she had given him the past two months. His team was responding to his leadership, and for the first time, he felt he was a part of developing a culture of employee engagement. He knew Hannah deserved much of the credit.

Seth looked down at his watch and realized he had some time before his employees showed up for work. He checked the schedule to see how many of his employees were working in the morning. Fifteen. That was enough. He looked at Hannah and said, "I've got to run an errand. I'll be back."

DOUGHNUTS ANYONE?

The noise in the call center was normally very consistent. Anyone who walked through the office during normal business hours would hear tapping on computer keyboards and call center reps talking to their customers.

Hannah was in Carmen's office when she heard the laughter. It was 8:30 now, so the call center was packed full of employees. The laughter from the reps was noticeably uncommon, so she got up to see what the commotion was all about.

Several of the employees were standing so they could look across the office. Hannah looked in their direction and found the source of their laughter. There he was. Seth was standing in the middle of the office in a tuxedo. He had a white cloth draped over his arm, and a silver tray full of doughnuts. He was walking through the office serving doughnuts to his team members. Not all the reps. Just his. This was his way of celebrating their success.

Hannah walked over to get a closer view, and noticed Seth was handing each of his employees a card as he served them breakfast at their desks. He met Hannah as she walked over to him. He lowered the tray and asked, "A doughnut for the boss?"

Hannah took a doughnut from the tray and moved closer to one of Seth's reps. She looked down to read the card he was passing out. It read, "Enjoy your doughnut. This is my way of saying thanks for everything you do. You make me proud to be your leader!"

Carmen had followed Hannah out of her office and was standing behind her with her arms crossed. She had a typical scowl on her face. "I'm sure this is screwing up our customer hold time. Everyone in the office is wasting time watching this spectacle."

Seth walked over to Carmen and held out the tray. "Can I interest you in a doughnut?"

She unfolded her arms, turned around and stormed back to her office. Seth's intention was to recognize his employees and celebrate their success, but in the process he'd managed to anger one of his peers. Carmen appeared to be mad that

his stunt had disrupted the office, but he suspected there was more to it. By recognizing his
team, he had just raised the bar for his fellow
managers.

At that point, Seth didn't care why Carmen was
mad. His employees weren't starving for doughnuts.
They were starving for attention, and Seth had given
them what they needed. At the same time, he communicated to his team that celebration was going to
be a part of the culture he developed.

MATTIE

Word about Seth's doughnut episode spread
quickly through the office. Seth had changed out
of his tuxedo that morning, but he had doughnuts
and cards in his office for the other employees
when they came in for their shift.

"Only you would go out and rent a tuxedo to
serve your team doughnuts for breakfast," Aaron
joked as he walked into Seth's office that afternoon.

"Actually, I didn't rent the tuxedo to serve
doughnuts," Seth laughed as he put down his
pen and turned toward Aaron. "I was in a wedding
on Saturday, and had it in my car to return today. I
just figured I'd get one last use out of it before it
went back."

"Outstanding! Now I'm going to be spending my
days trying to figure out how to beat that. Every
single person on my team has been asking when
they're going to be served breakfast at their desk."

Mattie walked to Seth's door as Aaron was
leaving. Her shift was about to start, so she had
missed the morning doughnuts.

"I know it's after lunch," she laughed, "but
where's my doughnut? I'm going to save it for
this afternoon."

Since Seth had arrived in January, Mattie hadn't said much to him. Other than his one-on-one meeting and the conversation they had about her attendance problem, he felt she was avoiding him. For her to walk in with a smile on her face and ask for her doughnut indicated she was as starved as the others for a little attention.

Seth motioned for her to take a seat and help herself to a doughnut. He handed her one of the cards, and told her he would be right back. Seth went to Carmen's office and asked her to schedule Mattie for a 15-minute meeting with him at the beginning of her shift. To Seth's surprise, Carmen agreed without causing a scene.

Seth had some time to review the January and February attendance reports before lunch, and he noticed Mattie had not missed a day of work in either of those months. He knew it was going to make the conversation he was about to have a lot easier.

"I thought you were going to save that doughnut for this afternoon," Seth joked as he walked back in his office and saw her putting the last piece in her mouth.

"Actually," she responded as she took a second doughnut from the tray, "I'm going to save *this* one for this afternoon!"

"Mattie, last year you had the worst attendance record of anyone on our team. I asked some of the other managers when I first got here what I should do, and some thought I should terminate you. The past two months you've had perfect attendance. Why the sudden turnaround?"

"I don't know," she said. "It just feels different since you got here. You tell us what's going on, and you treat us different than our last boss. She was nice, but she didn't walk around and say good morning. She didn't tell us what our results were every month. She certainly didn't serve us doughnuts at our desk. It wasn't a very fun place to come to work."

"Are you saying it has to be fun for you to come to work?"

"No," Mattie responded, "I'm not saying it has to be fun. I'm just saying it makes it a nicer place to be. And when you feel you're doing a good job and no one notices, it makes you think the work you do isn't very meaningful. It's just all different now."

"Well, let me first say I'm proud of your attendance record the first two months of this year. But let me also say this. As I mentioned in our last meeting, I expect you to be here when you're scheduled. It's not always going to be fun. There are going to be times you won't want to come to work. But I expect you to be here. In fact, if you have perfect attendance for the next four months, I'll treat you and your husband to dinner at the restaurant of your choice."

"Any restaurant?"

"Let me take that back," Seth smiled. "I'll treat you and your husband to dinner at any reasonably priced restaurant!"

"Fair enough."

Carmen walked to Seth's door and noticed Mattie was still in the meeting. "The fifteen minutes you asked for with Mattie are almost up. Do you need more time?"

"No," Seth answered, "we're done. She'll be right out."

Seth thanked Mattie again for her efforts, and told her he had confidence she would make it the next four months without missing a day. As she left, Seth realized he made progress with her by setting the expectation and communicating a positive consequence. He hoped she would respond so the next consequence wouldn't be negative.

Seth realized he also had made progress with Carmen. She didn't seem to be the same person who had charged into the conference room and ordered his employees back to work just two months earlier.

THE RESULTS ARE IN

The first thing Seth did that morning as he settled into his office around 8 o'clock was check e-mail. The first message he got was from Hannah. It read, "All managers in the conference room at 9 AM." They had just had their monthly management meeting, so Seth was curious why they needed to meet again.

It had been a couple weeks since Seth caused the stir with the doughnuts, but he was still getting harassed by his fellow managers in the conference room while they waited for Hannah. At 9 sharp, she arrived.

"Thanks for meeting on such short notice. As you all know, the company conducted an Employee Engagement Survey at the end of January. They got the feedback a few weeks ago, and just sent it out this morning."

"Do we still have jobs?" Jill joked as she looked at the other managers.

"Everyone but you," Hannah responded, "but I commit to you we'll do everything we can to help you find a new job."

Jill was stunned. The room fell silent.

"I'm just kidding!" Hannah laughed. "We actually did better than I thought we'd do."

"That wasn't even remotely funny," Jill shot back at Hannah with a glare.

Aaron replied, "I don't know. I got some humor out of it."

Jill threw her pen at Aaron, and Hannah began passing out the survey results.

"As you'll see," Hannah started, "there aren't any real surprises. As I said, we did pretty well in a few areas. We should be proud of that, and should work to ensure we continue doing those things well. If we're going to improve employee engagement and have it reflected on the December survey, we need to focus our efforts on improving those strength areas."

"What stood out?" Seth asked.

"A few things. First, employees don't feel they know what's going on. That is all about Directional Leadership and the issues we talked about at our first-quarter meeting. I assume you are all making progress on the four lessons we discussed, and I'm looking forward to hearing what you've done when we gather for our second-quarter meeting in a couple weeks."

"What else?" Jill asked.

"Recognition. Like all employees, they feel they work way too much and never get recognized for their efforts. We'll be talking about some of those solutions in Motivational Leadership in a couple weeks, and as long as we implement those ideas, we'll fix that area as well."

"What else?" Jill asked.

"Man, you're impatient!" Aaron remarked.

"The last big theme was the quality of the team," Hannah answered.

"What does that mean?" Carmen scowled.

"It's pretty common," Hannah replied. "The survey shows that employees think they are pulling their weight, but that the people around them are not."

"So what do we do?" Carmen asked, "Do we let them do all the hiring and firing now?"

"No, Carmen," Hannah replied calmly. "It just means we need to take a look at our team and make sure we have the right people in place to realize our vision. In fact, we'll be talking about those issues in Organizational Leadership in our third-quarter meeting."

"Where do we go from here?" Aaron asked.

"The first thing you need to do is schedule a meeting to share the results of the survey with your teams," Hannah answered. "Thank them for their input, and let them know you'll be working on the areas of concern."

"Any questions?" The room was silent as everyone read through the results.

"I've got a full day," Hannah said, "so I'm going back to my office. I should be here all day, so if anyone needs me, you know where to find me."

After Hannah left the conference room, Jill and Carmen followed her out. As Seth stood up to leave, Aaron motioned for him to sit back down. He walked over and closed the door, turned back to Seth and said, "I have an idea."

GREAT MINDS COME TOGETHER

"There is no way in the world I'm scheduling 50 people off at the same time," Carmen fumed as she glared at Aaron and Seth. "Customer hold time would go through the roof."

"Come on, Carmen," Aaron said. "It's just one hour. All we have to do is have the overflow calls routed to the Austin office for that one hour. It's as simple as that."

As Aaron was pleading his case, Hannah walked in.

"Did I not get my invitation to the meeting?" she laughed.

"I'm glad you're here," Aaron said. "Can you please talk some sense into Carmen?"

"What's the problem?" Hannah asked.

Seth jumped in. "Aaron and I want to have a joint team meeting to share the results of the survey. We anticipate it will take an hour. Since one of the issues is that our employees don't feel they know what's going on, we want to spend the next half hour talking about the vision of the organization and how they contribute to it. Ultimately, we'd be making the strategic plan available to everyone. It would be like a Town Hall Meeting."

"I think it's a great idea," Hannah responded. She turned to Carmen and asked, "What's the problem?"

"As I just explained to Aaron and Seth, our customer hold time would go through the roof."

"Our customer hold time wouldn't have to go through the roof," Hannah responded. "It will take some creativity with scheduling, and may require us to route the overflow calls to the Austin office for that one hour, but we can do it."

Aaron and Seth looked at Carmen with a look that said, "I told you so!"

Hannah continued. "It's been done before. Heck, we've closed the entire office for a Christmas party. We can certainly do it for this."

As difficult as she could be sometimes, even Carmen was smart enough to pick her battles. This was not one worth fighting.

THE SECOND-QUARTER MEETING

Seth had been looking forward to this meeting since January. He knew Hannah was going to introduce the four lessons related to Motivational Leadership, and he was anxious to hear what she had to say. If there was anything Seth did well, it was inspire his employees.

Everyone was seated at 8 AM ready to go when Hannah walked in.

"Let's get started," she said. "I promised you these meetings would be over by noon, and I'm hoping you have a lot to share before we start discussing Motivational Leadership. Who would like to start?"

Before Seth had the opportunity to speak up, Aaron jumped right in.

"I have something to share regarding preparing the organization for change. After our last meeting, I thought about how everyone hates to change. Although we may not like change, we all like to improve. And since the only reason the corporate office changed the strategic plan was to improve, I presented the changes as improvements. It may be small, but I figured I'd give it a shot."

Carmen rolled her eyes. She seemed to always roll her eyes if it wasn't something she thought of first.

Hannah responded, "I like it. It's small, but simple. Who else has an example of something they tried?"

After a long pause, Seth figured no one else was going to offer an example, so he decided to share his experience.

"My example has to do with recruiting support from the top 29 percent. I started by identifying my top 29 percent. I wanted to make them feel special, so I called them in for a meeting. I told them about the procedure change for Representative Occupancy, and asked for their input. After I dealt with their issues, I got their commitment."

"I like it," Hannah replied. "Did it make a difference?"

Hannah knew it had made a difference because Seth had shared his experience in her office after it happened. He figured she wanted him to share it with everyone else.

"Yes, it made a difference," Seth answered with a smile. "When I had my meeting with the entire team, my top 29 percent stood up and defended the change to the rest of the team. The whole experience was good."

"I certainly can't say the same," Jill said. "My team fought the change. In fact, they weren't on board when we left the meeting, but I reminded them they didn't have a choice."

"Did you recruit support from your top 29 percent?" Hannah asked.

"No, I didn't. You can rest assured I'll do it next time."

"Who else used lessons from Directional Leadership?"

No one offered a story, and Hannah didn't want to push.

"Some of you may think of a story as we go along, so feel free to share it," Hannah continued. "In the meantime, I want to make sure we have plenty of time to review Motivational Leadership, so let's move on."

Hannah had placed the two flipcharts at the front of the room prior to the meeting. One had her drawing of the puzzle pieces, and the other had the first four lessons of Engaged Leadership. In the second puzzle piece, she wrote the word *Motivational*.

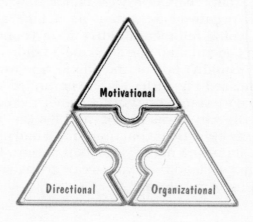

"We've been spending time throughout the first quarter exploring ways to build consensus toward the vision of the organization as Directional leaders. We can have the greatest vision for our company and communicate it better than anyone, but if we don't inspire people to want to pursue it, it won't matter. We have a responsibility to build a culture that motivates our employees to pursue the vision."

Hannah approached the flipchart that showed the first four lessons and added the fifth when she wrote:

5. Lead with positive motivation.

She sat back down. "This may sound simple, but it's not. From the time we were children, we've been led with negative motivation. As a little girl, my mother would tell me if I didn't do my homework, I couldn't go outside. She'd tell me if I didn't do the dishes, I couldn't talk on the phone. She would tell me if I missed my curfew, I'd be grounded."

"What's wrong with that?" Carmen asked dryly. "That's the way I was raised, and it's the way I'm raising my kids. Does that make me a bad parent?"

"No, it doesn't make you a bad parent. It's just that when we lead that way, we're giving someone something to run from."

"If it works, then what's the problem?" Carmen asked as she looked around the room for support.

Hannah sat in silence for a moment. Seth couldn't tell if she was annoyed by Carmen's questions and was trying to maintain composure, or if she was thinking of a response.

"What I'm trying to say is that we should be giving our employees something to run toward," Hannah continued. "And it's not hard to do. For example, instead of my mother telling me I couldn't go outside if I didn't get my homework done, she could have turned it around and told me I could go outside if I did my homework. Instead of telling me I couldn't talk on the phone if I didn't do the dishes, she could have told me I could talk on the phone if I did the dishes."

Aaron spoke up. "It almost sounds too simple, but it makes sense. It's like what Seth did with Mattie. He could have told her he would write her up the next time she was absent. Instead, he told her he'd treat her and her husband to dinner if she had four more months of perfect attendance."

"Exactly!"

Carmen didn't say a word.

Jill asked, "What's next?"

Hannah walked back to the flipchart and wrote:

6. Celebrate small successes.

"This one doesn't need much explanation at all," she said. "We simply don't celebrate enough."

"I'm going to have to disagree with you on that one," Carmen said. "We have quite a few celebrations around here."

Seth nearly fell out of his chair. Aaron looked at him with complete disbelief, and they both broke out laughing.

"You have got to be kidding me, Carmen," Aaron continued laughing. "When is the last time you've celebrated a small success with your team? Heck, when's the last time you celebrated a big success with your team?"

"We celebrate birthdays in the break room every month, and seem to celebrate just about every holiday. We are always spending money to celebrate something."

"That's not what I'm talking about," Hannah responded. "I'm talking about celebrating an accomplishment, not a date on the calendar."

"I assume you're talking about something like what Seth did with the doughnut fiasco," Carmen replied.

"Why was that a fiasco?" Seth asked.

"Because she didn't think of it first," Aaron replied, "and because it will require her to do the same."

"Who cares if Seth raised the bar on celebration?" Hannah asked. "Our employees told us in the Employee Engagement Survey that they don't get enough recognition. In one simple act of celebrating a small success, Seth got huge kudos from his team. They are still talking about it, and it happened weeks ago. That little 'fiasco' will pay dividends for some time."

The room was silent for a moment before Hannah continued.

"I'm not sure if Seth raised the bar or established the bar, but I encourage each of you to follow his lead and find ways to celebrate your small successes."

"Any questions?" After a moment of silence, Hannah said, "Good. Let's take a half-hour break. Go check your e-mail and voicemail, or do whatever it is you do when you take a break, just be back in thirty minutes. If you're not, you get to teach the next points. How about that for expectations and consequences!"

BACK FROM THE BREAK

As everyone filed back in the room five minutes early, Hannah was in her seat. As Seth sat down, he noticed Hannah had already written the next lesson on the flipchart. It read:

7. Encourage life balance for all employees.

She looked around the room and said, "Life seems to be moving at a faster pace than ever before. We have so many things happening, and we're expecting more from our employees than ever before."

Jill interrupted. "I think that goes for everyone around this table, too. If I don't work at least ten hours a day, I can't keep up."

"I agree," Aaron said. "If I leave early to go watch one of my daughter's games, I have to take work home and do it after I put the kids to bed."

"I understand," Hannah said. "We are all in the same boat. But you made an interesting point. As a manager, you have the luxury of being able to leave early and take work home with you. Our employees don't have that luxury."

"So what are we going to do now?" Carmen responded. "Are we going to start letting everyone come in late and leave early? This place would be a zoo."

"No, Carmen. I'm not suggesting our employees can have the same flexibility we enjoy as managers. We have a responsibility to have a certain number of reps on the phones at the times the company requires in order to provide adequate coverage for our customers."

"Then we don't have the ability to offer the same flexibility we enjoy as managers," Jill said. "That's fine with me. If they want it, they can get promoted and put in ten-hour or twelve-hour days like we do."

"So we shouldn't offer them any flexibility to encourage life balance since they're not in a management position?" Hannah asked.

"I don't think that's what she said," Carmen blurted out. "They've chosen to be in a job that requires them to work a certain shift. They knew that when they accepted the job."

"So people who work in a job that requires them to work a certain shift shouldn't expect any flexibility that might help balance their life?" Hannah asked.

"I have to jump in here," Seth interrupted. "I don't think we have to allow our employees to come and go as they please to be flexible. I think we just have to be willing to work with them when they need it."

"Exactly," Hannah said. "And it may require a shift in thinking for some of you. If you have an employee who wants to come in a little later, for whatever reason, and they've cleared it with you so we can cover their shifts, we should be willing to do it."

"No one ever did that for me," Jill frowned.

"And that's what I meant when I said it may require a shift in thinking for some of you," Hannah said. "Don't make decisions on flexibility based on what someone did with you. Make decisions on flexibility based on what you would have liked someone to do with you."

"Any questions?" After a moment of silence, Hannah walked back to the flipchart and wrote:

8. Create a fair work environment.

She sat back down and said, "This is the last lesson for today, and it's about our ability to create a fair work environment."

"There are laws that protect employees," Carmen sighed, "and we follow them all."

"I'm aware of the laws in place to protect our employees, and I fully expect us to follow each and every one of them. But I'm not talking about it from a legal sense. I'm talking about it from a leadership sense."

"What's the difference?" Jill asked.

"There are plenty of things we can do to be fair to employees that aren't required by law, and these are the things that engage the disengaged employee. Our employees are constantly comparing themselves to others. They compare how much money they make. They compare the rewards they get. They compare everything."

"As long as we treat everyone equally," Carmen replied, "then we should be just fine."

"I'm not talking about equal treatment," Hannah responded. "I'm talking about fair treatment. If our goal is employee engagement, then we must make employees feel they work in a fair environment. We simply can't expect an employee to feel engaged in the workforce when they feel they haven't been treated fairly."

"Fair treatment is pretty broad. Any suggestions?" Seth asked.

"There's one thing in particular I think you should do. Be consistent in the consequences you give. Your employees may look for fairness in pay and rewards, but they also want to know we're consistent and fair in enforcing the rules."

Carmen looked up and said, "It's noon."

"Yes, it is," Hannah said. "You've got the entire quarter to set this office on fire with Motivational Leadership. Go out there and make something big happen!"

THE POWER OF POSITIVE MOTIVATION

Seth made a point to get out of his office to visit with employees every day. Carmen warned him that he had set a precedent by serving his team breakfast at their desks, and that his employees would now expect him to spend money recognizing them. Seth discovered she was half right. It wasn't about the money he spent. It was about the attention.

He asked Jill one day why she didn't spend time in the call center with her employees. She explained she simply didn't have the time to "wander around" during the day, but then neither did Seth. He didn't have the time. He made the time.

A couple weeks after the second-quarter meeting, Seth was out making his morning rounds. He had just reviewed the March reports, and was somewhat disappointed. He held onto third place in attendance, and improved from fourth to third in a key quality measurement. A month ago he would have been thrilled with that progress, but Seth's competitiveness left him wanting more.

If Seth was raising the bar for his fellow managers, Aaron was proving he had no trouble getting over it. He was creating his own ways of recognizing his team, and had taken on Seth's habit of walking around visiting with employees every morning. He noticed Aaron didn't make it out that morning, and saw him sitting in his cubicle.

"Not up for your morning jog?" Seth laughed as he walked into Aaron's cubicle.

"Not today," Aaron said without looking up. "I have four reports due to Hannah by noon. But first, I've got to cover a performance review with an employee who will complete six months with the company next week."

Seth hadn't done a performance review at this point, so he thought it would be as good a time as any to learn. "Do you mind if I sit through the review so I can see how they're done?"

"I don't mind at all. In fact, I'm on my way to get the employee right now. It's Janie Davis. You've met her before. You can sit in that chair in the corner and observe."

When Aaron walked back into the office with Janie, Seth noticed a concerned look on her face. Aaron explained to her that Seth was observing the review so he could learn how to do them with his own employees. From the moment she sat down, Janie was staring directly at the floor, with her shoulders rolled forward and her head hung down.

Aaron began. "Janie, as you know, I am required to do a review with you now that you've been with us six months. You've been doing pretty well, but I need you to focus on a couple things. You always forget to tell the customer you're putting them on hold. Also, you never thank people for using Halifax. I need you to work on those two things for me."

"Yes, sir."

"Now," Aaron continued, "I'll be watching for these things in your monthly observations. If I don't see an improvement, I'll have no choice but to write you up and put it in your file. I have faith in you that you'll get the hang of it. Do you have any questions?"

"No, sir."

"Okay, then. If you'll sign at the bottom of this performance review, you can head back to work."

Janie signed the form and left his office. Her shoulders were rolled forward and her head was hanging down. Aaron turned to Seth with a look of relief that he'd completed the review.

"I hope that helped," Aaron commented. "Now, I've got to get these reports done for Hannah. Let's grab some lunch today."

"I can do lunch today. But before I leave, let's talk about the review. I don't want to be critical because I've never done one before . . ."

Aaron interrupted. "You're not going to tell me how I should have done the review, are you?"

"Absolutely not. I just noticed that she came in here looking dejected before you even said a word."

"They all come in here that way," Aaron said. "They're coming to see the boss."

"I just don't think coming to see the boss should be a bad thing. And it's one thing for them to come in here expecting something bad to happen, but I don't think they should leave here with the same dejected look on their face."

Seth had spent a lot of time getting to know Aaron, and he hoped their relationship was strong enough for this conversation. He believed the relationship was built on a foundation of trust. If it wasn't, Seth knew he may have just crossed a line.

After an uncomfortable pause, Aaron broke the silence. "If one of the other managers had just said that to me," Aaron smiled, "I would have thrown her out of my office, but I trust your opinion. What would you have done differently?"

Seth was relieved he hadn't offended Aaron. "First of all, like most employees, Janie came in here thinking she was going to hear what she was doing wrong, and she was listening for it. I thought you started out great telling her she was doing pretty well, but you jumped straight from that quick comment to telling her what she was doing wrong."

"But I needed to tell her what she was doing wrong."

"True. But she may have been more open to those ideas if you spent some time providing specifics of what you thought she was doing well. Maybe I'm wrong, but if it were me and I had an employee like Janie, I would spend 80 percent of my time in the review telling her what she was doing well, and 20 percent of my time telling her what she could do to improve."

"Anything else?" Aaron asked.

"I would have focused on some aspect of positive motivation. You had an employee you thought was doing a pretty good job, but you told her if she didn't improve, you would write her up and put it in her file. She's not running toward something, like Hannah talked about in positive motivation. She's running away from getting written up."

"You learned all that from Hannah's lesson?" Aaron laughed.

"No. I learned it by putting myself in the shoes of the employee. Every boss I've ever had threatened me with negative motivation. When Hannah mentioned leading with positive motivation, it just made sense."

Aaron and Seth spent some more time talking through the review, and Aaron agreed to bring Janie back in to share more of the things she was doing well. When Seth got back to his office, he realized two peers can teach each other when a foundation of trust is in place.

WINNER BY A NOSE

If there was anything Halifax did exceptionally well, it was train its employees. Seth enjoyed the opportunity to learn from Hannah, and considered the chance to attend formal training sessions a bonus.

Halifax University was created over a decade ago as a central training location, and all employees were encouraged to take advantage of it. Not only did the company encourage it, but Hannah pushed all her managers to register for training. A week earlier Hannah had gotten a call from the training center informing her of a last-minute cancellation for a presentations training workshop, and she offered Seth the opportunity to go. He jumped at the chance.

Seth was picking up his luggage in the baggage claim area that evening when his cell phone rang. He had just gotten back from the training session and was looking forward to going to his apartment to relax. But when Hannah called to meet at La Cantina, he figured relaxation would have to wait.

He didn't realize Aaron would be there. When he walked in, Aaron and Hannah watched him walk toward the table with smiles on their faces.

"What's all the smiling about?"

"April results came out while you were gone," Aaron replied.

"I got a call from Jill telling me one of my employees dropped the ball getting my team's results to her, so I thought there might be a delay. I asked Miles to take care of it for me while I was in training, and apparently he let me down. So much for empowerment."

"I took care of it for you," Aaron said.

"Then why didn't someone call me with the results?"

"We didn't call you because we wanted to see you face-to-face when you heard the news," Hannah replied.

"What news?"

"Your team is no longer in third place in attendance and quality," Aaron said. "They're in first."

Seth stared at Aaron as though it didn't register. He then turned and stared at Hannah. Neither said a word. They just sat and smiled.

Seth broke the silence. "Are you serious, or is this some sort of mean joke?"

"It's the real deal, my friend," Aaron said. "I've been in first place nearly every month since the office opened, and you just knocked me off the mountain. It was a photo-finish, but you won fair and square."

Seth was ecstatic. He hugged Hannah. He hugged Aaron. He even hugged the waitress when she brought their margaritas.

"It's not champagne, but it'll have to do," Hannah said as they raised their glasses. "To proof that a culture of employee engagement can truly make a difference."

Seth's team was measured in areas other than attendance and quality, but these were the areas that had shown significant improvement. He committed to Hannah that he would take his team from last place to first place in every area they measured within one year. He had gotten them to first place in two key measurement areas. In the back of his mind, he hoped to do it in six months. To everyone's shock, he did it in four. He enjoyed the moment while it lasted. He would soon find out that getting to the top was one thing. Staying on top was another.

A LESSON ON EMPOWERMENT

Seth couldn't wait to get back to the office the next day to share the good news with his team. As he opened the door to the call center, he looked across the office to his cubicle. He could see the hand-made banner in his cubicle. "Congratulations!" it read. As he walked through the office, several employees were giving him the thumbs-up sign. He looked toward Carmen's office and saw her standing in the doorway with her arms crossed. Mad again.

As he walked into his office, he could read the rest of the banner. Across the bottom were the words "From the #1 team in the office!" Each of his team members had signed the banner. Apparently someone else in the office couldn't wait to share the good news.

"It's pretty rewarding when the people who did the work recognize their boss, isn't it?" Hannah asked as she walked into Seth's office.

"I'm at a loss for words."

"It shows they appreciate your leadership," Hannah replied.

Seth sat quietly for a moment. "I know I should be wrapped up in the excitement of my team's results, but I can't get past the fact one of my employees dropped the ball on getting the reports to Jill. I've got to figure out how to deal with that."

Hannah walked over and sat down. "At our next quarterly meeting, I'll be addressing empowerment. In the meantime, just know it's all about culture, and it takes time."

"It just seems too simple to take time for empowerment to work. I mean, we want empowered employees, and I'm sure most employees want to feel empowered. If that's the case, how can an employee like Miles drop the ball?"

"There are several reasons," Hannah explained. "First, real empowerment requires the most enormous shift in thinking of any management practice in the workplace today. Most people lead others the way they were led, and it takes a pioneer to embrace the level of change needed to practice real empowerment. It requires that we give up the assumptions, behaviors, and processes that support the old system."

"So it really is about more than just giving people tasks to do."

"Absolutely," Hannah continued. "Real empowerment is based more on culture than tasks. In fact, it's based solely on a culture of trust. Since most people are practical and want a list of things to do after they've been through training or complete a book, many never get to the point where they are truly building a culture."

"So you're saying the only way an employee will take on responsibility is if he trusts the person who's asked him to do it?"

"No, that's not it," Hannah continued. "What I'm saying is that real empowerment has a chance of surviving when trust is in place. If I ask you to do something and I haven't built a culture of trust, then you may be afraid I'll punish you if you do it wrong, or embarrass you if you make a mistake."

"Carmen mentioned to me once that she doesn't delegate work to her employees because she knows they'll let her down."

Hannah lowered her voice. "Carmen doesn't delegate work to her employees because real empowerment requires the person to give up a significant amount of power. In the absence of a culture of employee engagement, the only tool many leaders have is position power. If Carmen hasn't built a culture where employees want to do the work, how can she get the work done if she gives away the very power that forces someone to do it?"

Seth sat for a moment to let the lesson sink in.

"I know Miles let you down when he dropped the ball," Hannah said as she leaned forward in her chair. "But remember that it probably has more to do with us than him. He probably has considerable respect for you, so let him know your concerns. He will probably work hard not to let you down in the future. But most importantly, just keep working on developing a culture of employee engagement. When you've achieved that, empowerment will have a chance to work."

Although some of Seth's success came from what he did right to build the right culture, much of it came from what he didn't do wrong to tear it down. Hannah had a way of showing up at just the right time to teach a lesson that kept him from committing some culture-killing acts. This was one of those occasions.

BELLS WILL BE RINGING

Seth and Jill had been meeting most of the morning. Although Carmen was the manager in charge of employee schedules, Jill was her backup. Hannah had asked Jill to ensure someone else in the office could do it in case they both were out of the office. Seth agreed to be the one.

Every twenty minutes or so, they would hear a bell ring in the office. The first two or three times they didn't think much of it, but when they noticed the call center reps were standing up to see what it was, they figured it was time to investigate.

They looked to see where everyone was staring, and it appeared to be Aaron's office, so they walked that way. Just before they got to his doorway, they heard the bell again. They looked inside and saw Aaron meeting with one of his employees. They were both laughing.

Not wanting to interrupt, Seth and Jill went back to her office. They figured Aaron would explain the bell ringing later.

After about an hour, Aaron walked into Jill's office. "It's working," he said with a smile.

"What's working?" Seth asked.

"The bell," Aaron replied. "I needed a way to celebrate the small successes of my team, and I chose a bell. Every time one of my team members does something to reach a goal they've set for themselves, they get to ring the bell. Not only is it a way to recognize them, but it raises the curiosity level of everyone else in the office."

"Yes, it does," Carmen said as she walked into Jill's office. "And in the process, it distracts our employees. I don't know what the bell ringing is about, but it's got to stop."

"Carmen," Aaron replied, "you have a way of throwing a wet blanket on every idea someone else comes up with. Let's walk back to my office, and I'll explain to you what all the bell ringing is about, and why it's not going to stop."

As he was leaving Jill's office, Aaron turned around to Seth and said, "Oh, and by the way, the bell does one other thing. It raises the bar on my good friend Seth. You see, as I was walking down here, two of your employees stopped me to ask why you don't ring a bell when they do something great."

"Outstanding," Seth laughed. "I love a little competition, and I'm up to the challenge. Game on!"

A LESSON IN LIFE BALANCE

Seth was from Texas, so he expected hot weather during the summer. He was hoping the unbearable heat would hold off until July or August, but June was bringing record temperatures. It seemed the heat put people in a bad mood. Particularly Carmen.

There weren't many mornings Seth wasn't one of the first managers to the office. He had gotten more involved with his church and just returned from a weekend retreat. It had been a particularly long weekend, and he'd been working some really long hours the week before, so he decided to stay in bed a little longer than usual that Monday morning. According to the May reports, his team held their positions in every category, so he felt things were moving along well.

When he got to the call center that morning, he noticed someone sitting at his desk. As he got closer to his cubicle, he realized it was Carmen. She was shuffling through the paperwork on his desk.

"Have you lost something?" Seth asked with a little contempt in his voice.

"It's nice of you to finally show up to work. I've been dealing with a problem all morning, and I got tired of waiting for you to get here."

Carmen continued to rifle through his desk as Seth stood in his doorway. "I have an idea," he said as he put down his briefcase. "Step away from my desk, and I'll be happy to find whatever it is you're looking for."

"I'm trying to find a vacation request one of your employees says you approved. It's Deanna Curtis. I have her scheduled to work tomorrow, and she came in claiming you signed off on her taking the day off. I told her that couldn't be the case because she hasn't been here long enough to accrue any vacation days. She said you authorized it."

"First of all, get up." Seth stood behind his chair until Carmen got up and stood next to his desk. He sat down and motioned for Carmen to sit in the guest chair she was leaning against.

"I appreciate you trying to take care of this issue," Seth started. "It could have waited until I got into the office, but since you're here, let's work through it. First of all, Deanna will celebrate her six-month anniversary with the company on Friday."

"I know. I checked her employment date. But the policy clearly states she's not entitled to vacation days until she's been here six months. That means she can't take days off until next week."

Seth stared at Carmen for a few seconds before he responded. "Do you have a gentle bone in your body? This office is not going to collapse because we allow Deanna to take a vacation day three days early."

"It's our job to enforce the policies of this company."

"The policies of this company are in place to ensure we have a structure by which to operate," Seth argued. "I would maintain it's not our job to enforce the policies. It's our job to use the policies to help guide our decisions when running this company. And that's exactly what I did, and exactly what I will do in the future."

"I'll take this up with Hannah."

"I think that would be a splendid idea," Seth smiled. "And while you're at it, explain to her that my employee's mother is going in for day surgery on Friday, and that she requested the day off to be with her family. Maybe you can explain to her that the employee agreed to come in early and leave late for the next week to make up the time since she knew she wasn't entitled to a vacation day yet, but that I told her I would make an exception, and that . . ."

Before Seth could finish his comment, Carmen got up and walked out of his office. For a moment he questioned his decision, and wondered if he'd done something wrong. Then he thought back to Hannah's lesson about encouraging life balance. He knew if he wanted his employees to be motivated enough to pursue the company's vision, he had to continue to work on the culture. And part of the culture for Seth would be a willingness to work with employees. He was willing to fight that battle any day.

THE THIRD-QUARTER MEETING

Seth was amazed the third-quarter meeting was here. He wasn't sure if the time was going by fast because there was so much work to do, or if he was just enjoying the job.

Throughout the second quarter, Seth had seen several ideas implemented to celebrate the small successes in the office, and he was looking forward to hearing what everyone had to say. He initially planned to tell everyone about his ideas, but he was pretty certain they knew exactly what he'd been doing.

Everyone but Aaron was sitting in the conference room when Hannah walked in. The clock read 7:55. Hannah just smiled. "I almost stopped to wash my car earlier this week, but I just knew one of you would be late today. It just may be Aaron."

Aaron ruined her fun. "I'm here. I'm here," he shouted as he rushed into the room.

"You almost didn't make it," Seth laughed.

"I had to pick up the cake for the Fourth of July party at lunch, and it wasn't ready," he said as he tried to catch his breath. "But I made it."

After Aaron got seated and Hannah got situated at the head of the conference table, she slowly looked around the table at each manager. She paused as she looked into the eyes of each manager and smiled.

"This past quarter was very rewarding for me," Hannah said. "I anticipated it would take a full year to start seeing a change in the culture, but it's already starting to happen. I know it hasn't been easy, and I know you're working more hours than you were before I got here. I hope you see the hours you're spending now developing the culture as an investment in the future of your team."

For the first time, Hannah saw all four heads around the table nodding in agreement. Even Carmen was coming around. Or at least she was pretending.

"Now then," Hannah continued, "I don't need to hear about the things you did to celebrate your small successes because I've been made aware of them by your teams. However, who would like to share something you did with one of the other lessons we learned last quarter?"

Seth always had a story to tell and was eager to share his experiences with the rest of the team. He was starting to learn that sometimes it's better to let someone else have the stage, and he sat back and waited.

Aaron chimed in first. "Let's talk about this positive motivation thing," he said. "I let Seth sit in while I did a six-month performance review on an employee back in April. I reviewed the employee's performance just like I've always done."

"And I appreciate you letting me sit in," Seth interrupted.

"No problem. But here's the deal, and this is hard for me to say. Seth sat with me so he could learn how to do a review, and I think I was the one who learned the most."

Everyone sat quietly as they waited for Aaron to continue.

"For years I have been doing these performance reviews, and I always did them the way my boss did them when I was a rep. I used to hate getting reviewed because I always knew I'd get beaten up, regardless of how well I did. My boss would always

find something wrong and point it out. I realized I
followed in the footsteps of my old boss."

"Do you mean you always looked for the things
they were doing wrong?" Jill asked.

"Yes. I actively looked for something they were
doing wrong. I thought that's what I was supposed to do, and it's what I did with this
employee. Ultimately, I got it turned around after
Seth brought up some valid points, but it was an
eye-opening experience concerning positive
motivation."

"Is Seth your own little personal coach now?"
Carmen commented.

"No, Carmen. But I also learned in that experience that we all have something to learn from
each other if we'll put down our guards long
enough to realize it."

"Great lesson," Hannah said. "Who else has
something to share?"

Hannah didn't expect her managers to be anxious to share stories at this point. She knew that
while they were building a culture with their
teams, she was building a culture with them. No
one knew better than Hannah that building a
culture takes time.

"Let's move on to the final aspect of Engaged
Leadership. Our meeting will be shorter than normal. I have an obligation at 10:30, so we won't be
taking a break this morning, and we may move
rather quickly through some of the information. If
you have questions after the meeting, I'll be happy
to make myself available."

Hannah had once again set up the flipcharts at
the front of the room prior to the meeting. On one
she had her drawing of the puzzle pieces, and on
the other she had the first eight lessons of Engaged
Leadership. She approached the drawing of the

puzzle pieces. In the third puzzle piece she wrote the word *Organizational*.

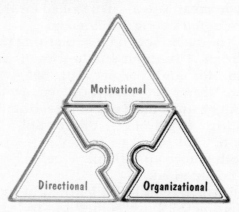

"We started the first quarter discussing our responsibilities as Directional leaders. We learned the four lessons that will help us build a consensus for the vision. We then discussed our responsibilities as Motivational leaders. We learned the four lessons that will help us inspire the team to pursue the vision. And now we'll discuss our responsibilities as Organizational leaders, and learn the four lessons that will help us develop the team to realize the vision."

She turned to the flipchart with the first eight lessons and added the ninth when she wrote:

9. Identify and position the appropriate talent.

She sat back down. "When we look at the three aspects of leadership in the model, we can all identify one area that we are better at than others."

Seth jumped in. "I'm definitely better at Motivational Leadership than Directional Leadership. I'm pretty good at building consensus, but I'm definitely more comfortable inspiring my team."

Aaron chimed in. "I'm just the opposite. I enjoy inspiring my team, but I'm definitely better at building consensus for the vision. Even more than that, I'm always thinking about the future, and trying to come up with new ways of doing things."

"Can you imagine if we had an entire team of visionaries?" Hannah asked. "Everyone would want to plan the future and build consensus toward the vision, but no one would have the ability to inspire the team. Or how about if we had an entire team of managers like Seth who were really great at inspiring the team, but weren't sure how to develop the team as a whole? We have a responsibility to focus on individuals, but we also have a responsibility to develop the team so the organization is bigger than certain employees."

Jill asked, "What's next?"

Hannah walked back to the flipchart and wrote:

10. Build a bridge between the generations.

"I suppose you mean we need to adjust to these spoiled little brats," Carmen said in her most sarcastic tone.

"I think it means we need to adjust to old people like you," Aaron laughed.

"I'm not that old. I just turned 54."

Seth laughed silently and slowly covered his mouth. "My mother isn't that old."

Everyone laughed. "Careful, Seth," Hannah replied. "I turn 51 later this year."

"How old are you, Seth?" Jill asked.

"I turn 24 in a couple months."

"I have socks older than you," Carmen frowned.

"You should probably think about getting some new socks," Aaron laughed.

Aaron and Jill were in the middle. They were both 35, and had been hired by the company as call center reps when they were younger than Seth.

"What I mean by building a bridge between the generations is we're all different," Hannah said. "We all grew up at different times, and our values are different. We have to be able to adjust to that, and not allow the generational differences to get in the way."

"That's hard for me to do," Carmen said. "For instance, when I grew up, my parents started work at 8 o'clock, and they didn't leave until 5. Period. They didn't show up late if they were tired, and they certainly didn't ask for time off early. I do the same thing, and it's annoying to watch Seth wander in here whenever he wants."

"But he stays long past 5," Aaron chimed in. "He doesn't have kids, so while we're at home taking care of kids, he's up here working."

"Keep in mind that the generational thing doesn't just apply to us," Hannah said. "You have several different generations on your teams, and you need to adjust to them as well. I have some information on the generations in my office, and I'll e-mail it to all of you. In the meantime, just be tolerant of generational differences."

Hannah walked back to the flipchart and wrote:

11. Move toward real empowerment.

She sat back down and said, "This next lesson is about our ability to empower our employees."

"Finally," Carmen sighed, "something I can agree with. We need to be giving some of this work to our employees. Delegation is the key."

"It's interesting you would say that because empowerment is perhaps the least understood of most management practices," Hannah said.

"It's pretty simple to me," Carmen replied. "Give someone a task and get out of the way!"

"That sounds great because on the surface it seems simple. If we give people more responsibility, then they're empowered. If we give people the power to make decisions, then they're empowered. But it's not that simple. For empowerment to work, we must have a culture in place that allows people to fail without the fear of being knocked down. Quite frankly, I don't think that culture exists here yet. It will if we follow each aspect of Engaged Leadership and build a culture of employee engagement."

"What do we do in the meantime?" Aaron asked.

"I would suggest you do a couple things. Start with giving your employees more information. For empowerment to work, employees need information. If I empower one of you to take on a task for me, you're going to gather all the information available to get it done. Too often we're protective of our information and don't share it with our employees. Give them more information so that when the culture is ripe for empowerment, they'll feel they have the information to take on more responsibility."

"Anything else?" Seth asked.

"Yes," she answered, "there is one last thing you can do related to empowerment. Stop solving all their problems. The one thing I've noticed since I got here is we solve too many problems for our employees. We don't challenge them to think through their own problems. If we don't turn them into thinkers, they'll never be ready to take on more responsibility through empowerment."

Hannah walked back to the flipchart and wrote:

12. Establish a strategy to maintain success.

"This is the last lesson for today. How many of you can tell me who you've been grooming to take your job if you get run over by a bus tomorrow?" Hannah asked.

No one said a word. Aaron broke the silence, "I personally look both ways before I cross the street in hopes of never getting run over by a bus."

Everyone laughed.

"You know what I mean. Something could happen to any of us. People get promoted. They get transferred. They retire. We have a responsibility to ensure life goes on around here without us, and that all the good work we've been doing is carried on. Our presence here shouldn't be required, and it won't be required if we establish a strategy to maintain success. Any questions?"

"Are you referring to a succession plan?" Carmen asked.

"That is certainly a good example of a strategy to maintain success. You've each worked awfully hard; it'd be a shame to let someone else take over who may not be up to the task of filling your shoes and carrying on the work you've done with your teams. Any other questions?"

"What's the fourth piece to the puzzle?" Seth asked.

"You'll find out at the fourth-quarter meeting in October. Any other questions?"

Seth needed more information on the last lesson, but it was obvious Hannah was in a hurry to end the meeting. He wasn't about to open his mouth and keep everyone else from getting out early. He decided he would hold his questions until later.

"The reason I am leaving early today is I'm expecting a call from my boss, Ross Harrison. He's noticed our office results have improved significantly the past six months, and he told his boss about us. Her name is Amanda Suttle, and she wants to come down here to see what we're doing."

"We've never been visited by a corporate vice president before," Aaron said. "Are you going to give her a presentation of what we've been doing?"

"No. You will."

Hannah had a way of bringing total silence to the room.

"I will?" Aaron asked.

"All of you. Your teams have produced the numbers, and you've led your teams. I'm not about to take credit for your work. You made the effort, and you're going to have an opportunity to strut your stuff in front of the big boss. She'll be here two weeks from Friday. I'll give out presentation assignments soon. In the meantime, you know the routine. Go out and have a great quarter. Let me know if you need any help."

With that, the final four lessons of Engaged Leadership had been taught. Seth had a feeling there wouldn't be much effort made over the next few weeks to implement the last four lessons. Everyone would be focused on the visit from Amanda Suttle.

Seth was glad he took advantage of the presentations training workshop back in May.

THE BIG BOSS

Seth had no idea so much effort could go into planning for a visit from an officer of the company. In fact, nearly every available minute for two and a half weeks in July was spent making preparations. Seth wondered if these executives would ever make visits if they had any idea how much it cost the company in preparation time alone.

Since Seth's team had once again held its position on the monthly reports for June, he felt he could spend some time getting ready for the meeting. This was not just any meeting. Not only was this to be the first visit to this call center by a corporate vice president, she was coming to examine exactly what it is they've been doing that has led to their recent successes.

Since these visits didn't happen very often, everyone was surprised when Hannah didn't spend the entire day meeting with Amanda on her own. Everyone but Seth. He knew Hannah's commitment to the development of her team, and this was her opportunity to put managers in front of a company executive.

Each manager was assigned a specific area of improvement to present. Seth didn't get nervous very often. He certainly wasn't nervous about his presentation. However, he was nervous about his task before the presentation. Hannah had asked him to pick up her boss from the airport.

"How do you people live like this?" These were the first words out of Amanda Suttle's mouth as she approached the company car sitting at the curb outside the airport. "It has to be 150 degrees out here. I hope the air conditioner works in that thing," she laughed as she approached the car.

"It does, ma'am," Seth replied as he opened her car door, "and we're only an hour from the office."

After Seth closed her door and ran around to get in the driver's seat, Amanda turned to him with a smile and said, "Call me ma'am again and you're walking to the office. My name is Amanda. And I am a grown woman, and can open my own car door."

"Sorry, Amanda. I was born and raised in Texas, and my mother . . ."

Amanda interrupted, "I know, I know. Your mother taught you it's a sign of respect. I may live in New Jersey, but I was born in Texas. I appreciate the gesture."

Amanda Suttle was nothing like Seth imagined. He expected her to be uptight and formal. She had a way of making Seth feel at ease. In fact, for the entire ride to the call center, they never even talked about business. They visited like they'd been friends for years.

DOWN TO BUSINESS

Everyone knew they had spent way too much time preparing their presentations for Amanda's visit. In fact, Seth was concerned the teams would feel neglected during that two-week period. He was surprised at first to see how much support he got from his team. After he gave it a little thought, it made sense. This wasn't just his presentation. They were as much a part of it as anyone, and they were proud of what Seth was going to present. In a nutshell, they had become engaged.

Hannah spent the morning with Amanda. From time to time, she would come out of her office to get some call center reps. She'd take them in her office and close the door. Even though they were doing a good job building a culture of employee engagement, the managers still got a little nervous knowing one of their employees was sitting in a closed office with their boss and her boss.

After a quick lunch, they all gathered in the conference room. Each manager had one full hour to make a presentation and to answer questions from Amanda. Although they may have spent too much time preparing their presentations, it paid off by the end of the day.

"I've been visiting call centers this year to see what kind of progress we're making on employee engagement," Amanda said. "There are some offices doing a nice job, but I can honestly say I've been the most impressed with what I've seen here. You're not just talking about it. You're making it happen. Hannah shared with me the model of Engaged Leadership, and explained you are implementing the ideas in your day-to-day activities. The key to your success is following a model, and I applaud you for that."

Amanda paused for a moment and looked around the room to allow her words to sink in.

"Your presentations were outstanding. You have a lot of potential in this office, and I wish you the best of luck for the remainder of the year."

After a full day of presentations, Amanda's mind was focused on business on the return trip to the airport. Seth had the opportunity to drive her back to the airport, and enjoyed the entire hour hearing more of her observations.

"What do you think of Hannah?" she asked Seth.

"I think she's awesome, and I don't know how she does it. She really spends more of her day leading her four managers than doing management stuff. She's constantly teaching us something, which we then apply to our teams, if we're smart. If it works, which it normally does, our results improve."

"I want to encourage you to do two things for me," Amanda pleaded. "One, learn as much as you can from Hannah while you're here. Her style of management is the exception, not the rule. And two, promise me you'll take those lessons and become the kind of leader Hannah is to you. We need more leaders like Hannah, and you have the chance to pass it on to others."

"I promise you I'll do both, Amanda," Seth said as they pulled up to the airport.

As she got out of the car, she turned around and looked at Seth. Before she closed the door, she said, "Forget the Amanda thing. From now on, call me Mandy."

Seth didn't know if the fact they were fellow Texans helped create the bond or if she was genuinely impressed with Seth, but he felt he was making a connection. He hoped it might help somewhere down the line.

FOUR REASONS PEOPLE FAIL

It was August now, and the corporate vice president's visit was over. That was the good news. The bad news was the July report had just come out and Seth's team had dropped to second place in attendance. Nothing of great concern, but Seth wanted to stay on top. He hoped it was just the distraction of Amanda's visit that had thrown everyone off.

Hannah always beat Seth to La Cantina. For the first time, Seth was the first to arrive. He needed to think through a problem he was having with an employee, and figured he'd do his thinking at La Cantina before his meeting with Hannah.

The waitress was bringing Seth his second margarita when Hannah walked in.

"Well, well, well," Hannah remarked as she walked over to the table with a grin on her face. "This is a first. You beat me here, and it looks like you got started without me."

"I needed some quiet time to think," Seth replied. "I figured I'd come over early."

"Good for you," Hannah replied. "Did you solve your problems, or are you going to need a few more margaritas for that?"

"I figure somewhere between the margaritas and your advice, I'll find my answers. My car is in the shop, and I'm taking a cab home. Bring on the margaritas!"

Hannah sensed the first margarita was already going to Seth's head. After she sat down, Seth explained the challenge he was having with Larry Marcus, a longtime Halifax employee. One of the key measurements in the office was called the First Resolution Rate, which measured the percentage of calls completed with a single contact. Since customers don't like being transferred around, upper management put a high priority on completing calls with a single contact. Larry's percentage was the lowest in the entire office, and it was keeping Seth's group from moving from second to first place. Seth explained he'd done everything he knew to do. He'd set expectations. He'd set positive consequences. He'd set negative consequences. Nothing had worked, so he was considering termination.

Hannah looked at Seth and said, "I'm about to teach you one of the best lessons you'll ever learn, so pay attention. There are only four reasons people fail. They fail because they lack one of these four things: skill, knowledge, resource, or motivation."

Hannah looked at Seth for a few seconds to ensure it was sinking in.

"Now, if you have an employee who can't seem to resolve a client's issue on the first call, is that a lack of skill?" Hannah asked.

"It could be if he doesn't know how to do it," Seth replied, "but Larry's been with the company for fourteen years. Twelve of those years he's been a call center rep, and there haven't been that many changes that would keep him from being able to handle client issues. According to his file, every time a change was implemented, he was trained. So in his case, it is not a lack of skill."

"Is it a lack of knowledge?" she asked.

Seth thought about Hannah's question for a moment and responded, "I suppose it could be if he didn't know what was expected of him, but I've made my expectations and consequences very clear. He's just not responding. So in his case, it is not a lack of knowledge."

"Okay," Hannah responded. "Is it a lack of resource?"

"Larry has everything he needs, so in his case, it's not a lack of resource."

"Seth," she asked, "If it's not a lack of skill, knowledge, or resource, what's left?"

"A lack of motivation," Seth replied.

"Exactly," Hannah replied. "You have an employee who's not resolving client issues on the first call because he's not motivated. What have you done as his leader to motivate him?"

"We do pay him every two weeks, don't we?" Seth laughed.

"Yes," Hannah replied with a smile. "But getting a paycheck to pay the bills doesn't motivate most employees, and it's obvious your positive and negative consequences aren't working. You need to find a way to motivate him before you can fire him."

"How do I do that?" Seth asked.

"I don't know, hotshot," Hannah replied. "That's for you to figure out. Give it some thought. Just know that the goal must not be to fire people. It must be to find ways to keep them. Not only is it less expensive, it's the compassionate thing to do."

Seth and Hannah spent the next hour or so talking about Amanda's visit, and what impact it would have on the other managers. After she left, Seth stayed a while and solved all his problems while enjoying another margarita. It was a relaxing ride home in the cab.

A LESSON IN CHARACTER

Seth's visit to Tucson started out less than smoothly. He had just arrived at the Tucson International Airport on a Tuesday afternoon and he was having a hard time doing what he'd done a million times when leaving an airport: opening the door to a taxi. The cab driver was nice enough to put Seth's suitcase in the trunk. Then he came around to try to get the back door open so Seth could get in the car. After several attempts and a grumble or two, he finally got it open and they were off to the hotel.

Seth was excited to be in Tucson on this September day, substituting the dry heat of Arizona for the humidity of Texas. The next morning he was going to start a financial management training session. Although he was excited to be learning what he needed to know about financial management, he wasn't looking forward to being away from his team for a week.

As Seth sat back to enjoy the half-hour drive, he noticed the cab driver was listening to a talk-radio show. It was an election year, and the discussion on the radio was surrounding a candidate who had confessed to some indiscretions in his personal life. Apparently he'd had an affair and hadn't been paying taxes on a housekeeper he recently hired.

From the backseat, Seth could hear the cab driver mumbling about what he was hearing on the radio. He looked at the cab license hanging on his visor and noted the driver's name was Barry. Barry looked at Seth in his rearview mirror and said, "Can you believe this? This bucket-head seems to be more concerned with what's going on in this guy's personal life than what he's going to do when he's elected. I just don't get it."

It was a local race, and Seth wasn't familiar with the candidate, but he was curious about Barry's comment. So he asked him, "What is it that you don't get?"

"I don't understand why everyone is so concerned with this guy's personal life. What he does in his personal life is none of my business. I'm just concerned with how he does his job."

Barry was not the first person to ever express this opinion to Seth. In fact, throughout much of his young life, Seth had heard many people attempt to separate their personal life from their professional life. While Seth had no desire to disrupt his pleasant cab ride to the hotel, his need to hear more from Barry took over.

"Barry, let me ask you a question," Seth started. "Do you believe someone can lack integrity in his personal life, but suddenly have integrity in his professional life?"

"Absolutely," Barry responded. "If he tells me he can, then I believe him!"

At this point, Seth's desire to get to the hotel was stronger than his desire to enter a debate with his cab driver. Barry and Seth were going to agree to disagree on this subject, and Seth looked out the window in an attempt to enjoy the remainder of his ride.

After his arrival at the hotel, Seth had a few hours to relax before dinner. In the office, there never seemed to be a spare minute to do anything other than dive headfirst into a pile of work.

He decided to spend his free time now considering his options for the lessons he still needed to apply before the fourth-quarter meeting.

A RETURN TO HER ROOTS

"I need you in the conference room for a quick huddle," Hannah said as she stuck her head into Seth's office. "It won't take more than fifteen minutes. I'm gathering up the other managers right now."

Carmen was the last one to show up. As she closed the door behind her, she looked at Hannah with her trademark frown, "What's this all about? I've got a ton of work to do since we're going to be out of the office for the quarterly meeting tomorrow."

Although all eyes were on Hannah, Jill spoke up. "I appreciate you dropping what you were doing to be here. I promise this won't take long."

Everyone turned toward Jill, wondering why she was the one leading the conversation. Seth could tell she was nervous since she stared at the table for a few seconds before she began.

"As you all know, I was a call center rep my entire career before I became a manager. In fact, I was a good call center rep."

"The best," Aaron responded.

"I got a lot of satisfaction being a rep. As we've talked about employee engagement, I think I was one of the most engaged reps in the office . . ."

She paused for a moment and let those words linger in the air.

". . . but I'm the first to admit I'm not very engaged as a manager. I seldom share anything in the quarterly meetings because I haven't implemented anything worth sharing. As we've worked to build a culture of employee engagement, I've realized I won't ever be engaged as a manager. I've talked to Hannah and told her I want to go back to being a call center representative effective the first of January."

You could have heard a pin drop. Everyone just sat in silence for a full minute.

Carmen was the one to speak up first. "Are you sure you want to do this? You worked so hard to get promoted, and now you're willing to throw it all away."

"First of all, I don't think I'm throwing anything away because I didn't work hard to get promoted. In fact, I never even asked to be promoted. When there was a management vacancy at this new office, I didn't get promoted because I was the best person for the job. I was promoted because I was the most effective call center rep, and that's the wrong reason to promote someone."

"You're okay with it?" Aaron responded.

"Okay with it?" Jill laughed. "It was my decision. This is not a bad thing, and it's certainly no reason to be sad. In fact, we should be celebrating. I'm going to return to something I love to do, and you get to find a manager who is engaged and excited to be on the team."

Seth was never all that impressed with Jill, but he'd always known her as a manager, and knew it would be difficult seeing her as a rep. But he was smart enough to know if she was going back to what she did best, he wanted her on his team.

"I assume it would be odd for you to join the team you've been managing," he said. "If you're looking for a new team, I'd love to have you."

"Thank you, Seth. I would like that very much."

"Okay, here's the deal," Hannah responded. "No one in this office knows about this, and I don't want anyone to know about it until the announcement is released tomorrow after the quarterly meeting. You are free to go back to work, and I'll see you tomorrow morning for the quarterly meeting."

Seth knew this would be one of the toughest quarterly meetings yet.

THE FOURTH-QUARTER MEETING

Every month when Seth paid his rent, he always spent time visiting with the apartment manager. When he approached her about having the management team's quarterly meeting in the apartment complex's clubhouse, she thought it was a great idea.

Because the clubhouse had a kitchen, Aaron and Seth decided to surprise everyone by cooking breakfast. Seth enjoyed cooking and had gotten a lot of practice since he didn't have anyone around to cook his meals.

Hannah and Carmen walked in together. "What's all this?" Hannah asked as she watched Aaron putting out the place settings.

"Breakfast," Seth replied with a smile. "My mother always taught me that breakfast was the most important meal of the day, and I figured we better get started with a full belly."

Seth saw Carmen digging through her purse. She looked at Hannah and said, "I have just enough Rolaids for the two of us."

Seth threw a towel at Carmen and said, "Just for that, you get to clean the dishes."

"Should I set a place for Jill?" Aaron asked.

"I assume she'll be here," Hannah replied. "Her job change isn't effective until the first of January, and she'd have to explain to everyone in the office why she's not here."

Jill was the only person who'd ever had to wash Hannah's car as a result of being late to a manager's meeting. She didn't like having to do it then, and she certainly didn't want to repeat the humiliating task.

"I'm not late, am I?" she said as she ran into the clubhouse one minute before 8 o'clock. "I refuse to let one of my last acts as a manager be washing Hannah's car."

"You're not late," Aaron laughed. "In fact, you're just in time for one of the best breakfasts you've ever had. The men are treating you to breakfast."

Jill had a look on her face as if to say, "You have got to be kidding me." She looked at Hannah and Carmen. They both shrugged their shoulders and smiled.

"Let's eat," Hannah suggested. "After we're done, I have a surprise for you."

After Jill's announcement the day before, Seth wasn't in the mood for any more surprises.

SOMETHING DIFFERENT

"I have asked Aaron to lead the meeting today," Hannah stated as everyone was getting settled for the meeting. "I've run the last three, and thought you might like to have someone else take the lead. Also, today will be a short meeting, and you'll have the rest of the day off. Do whatever you'd like."

Seth appreciated the day off, but wondered if anyone was thinking what he was thinking. Why Aaron? Seth liked Aaron, but he had a hint of jealousy that Hannah hadn't picked him.

"Okay," Aaron started as he pulled a stack of papers from his briefcase. "Hannah taught the twelve lessons of Engaged Leadership. In the second quarter, we discussed what we did to implement the four lessons in Directional Leadership, and in the third quarter, we discussed what we did to implement the four lessons in Motivational Leadership. Today, we're going to do two things."

Aaron passed out a sheet with all twelve lessons listed on it. "Since we don't have a flipchart here, I printed out the twelve lessons on a single sheet. We're going to start out talking about what we did to implement the four lessons in Organizational Leadership. Then we're going to reveal the fourth piece to the Engaged Leadership puzzle."

"Are we going to talk about how we're going to replace Jill?" Carmen blurted out. "I have someone in mind for that position."

"That is not part of today's agenda," Hannah chimed in. "I'll let you know when we'll be discussing that issue."

"Let's start by discussing the four lessons from Organizational Leadership," Aaron said as he tried to get control of the meeting. "Who has a story they'd like to tell?"

"I gave some thought to letting people know where they stand," Seth said. "I was telling my employees every month how they were doing, but I didn't really have a system in place. I took the goals they set for themselves at our first one-on-ones and had them printed on a 3-by-5 card, with a blank line next to each goal. Every month I provide my employees with a new card with the previous month's results. By doing this, there should never be a surprise when the annual performance review is done."

"Outstanding," Aaron responded. "I like the idea for two reasons. One, it's a constant reminder of how they're doing. But two, it's a system that can be passed along to someone else after you're gone, which puts in place a procedure to maintain the success of your team. Anyone else have something they'd like to share?"

When no one offered up another experience, Aaron pulled out a sheet of paper with the drawing of the puzzle pieces. He wrote two words in the fourth puzzle piece, and held it up for everyone to see.

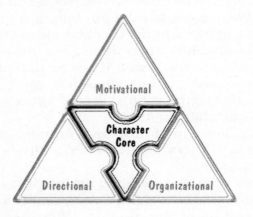

When he was certain everyone had seen it, Aaron put the sheet down on the table. "Character Core: Last week I asked Hannah why we hadn't talked about character at all in the model, and she shared with me that it isn't a part of one of the three aspects. It's a part of all aspects of Engaged Leadership, and is located at the center of the model."

"If you're talking about integrity, you're wasting your time," Carmen said. "We all have integrity, and we each manage our teams that way."

"I would agree that we operate our teams that way," Aaron replied, "but I don't think we're wasting our time talking about it. In fact, I think too many organizations assume their leaders lead with integrity and don't believe they need to talk about it. These are the companies whose leaders get led away in handcuffs."

"I guess these people need to be put through a course on business ethics," Jill responded. "They seem to make some pretty lousy decisions."

"They do make some pretty lousy decisions," Hannah chimed in, "but these decisions aren't due to a lack of business ethics. They're due to a lack of personal ethics. Companies don't make decisions. People make decisions. If someone lies and steals at home, they'll lie and steal at work. You can't separate the two."

"It seems some people believe there's a difference," Seth jumped in. "In fact, I met a cab driver in Tucson who believes someone can lack integrity in his personal life, but suddenly have integrity in his professional life."

"That cab driver was wrong," Hannah replied. "You either have character or you don't."

"I don't think anyone will be dragging us off in handcuffs," Carmen interjected. "We're not making decisions at our level that can have that much impact."

"That's probably true," Hannah said. "But I encourage you to keep in mind that your employees are watching you every day. They think they know your character, and they're looking for congruency in what you say and what you do."

"I don't think I understand," Jill admitted.

Hannah was about to give an example when Aaron jumped in first. After all, this was his meeting to lead.

"Let's use family as an example. If you tell your team that family is very important, but you work fourteen hours a day and every weekend, then you're sending a message that's not congruent with your character. If you tell your team that flexibility is important, but you aren't willing to bend when they need to leave an hour early and you have the people to cover the workload, then you're sending a message that's not congruent with your character."

"Congruency is the key," Hannah added.

Everyone sat around letting the lesson sink in.

"Hannah mentioned this would be a short meeting," Aaron stated, "and it will be. I have two more things to cover. One, let me remind you that the follow-up to the Employee Engagement Survey is coming up in December. We still have one final quarter to continue building on our culture of employee engagement. And two, as Hannah mentioned, we have the rest of the day off. You can do whatever you want. Go back to work, go home, go to the mall and buy me a present for my birthday next month . . . whatever you want. However, I'm buying dinner for anyone who shows up at La Cantina at 6 o'clock tonight. I hope you all can make it."

Seth never considered himself a workaholic, but he began to wonder about that when he chose to go back to the office instead of enjoying a free day off. He couldn't get Aaron's comment out of his head . . . one final quarter to continue building on the culture of employee engagement. How could there be only one more quarter?

THREE AMIGOS

When Aaron invited everyone to meet at La Cantina, Seth hoped it would be the first time the entire team got together in a social environment. As he suspected, Carmen came up with an excuse not to make it. Jill lived far from La Cantina, and since she decided to spend the rest of the day at home, she couldn't be there either. It ended up being just Seth, Aaron, and Hannah. The three amigos.

"I assumed everyone would be here," Hannah said, "so I saved this quick announcement for tonight. But since you are the only two here, I'll tell you. I'm taking next week off. I have a quick meeting in New Jersey, and then my husband and I are going to spend the rest of the week in New York."

"Can I go with you?" Aaron asked.

"No, you can't. In fact, that was the announcement I was going to make. I'm putting you in charge for the week."

Aaron and Seth turned and glanced at each other with a look of surprise. Seth was excited for Aaron, but he also was somewhat envious.

"Do I get to make any major changes?" Aaron asked. "There are a few personnel changes I'd like to make."

"No, you don't get to fire Carmen."

"It was worth a try," Aaron laughed.

"It was certainly an interesting question. Just out of curiosity, if I did give you the authority to make major changes, what would they be?" Hannah asked.

Aaron thought about it for a moment. "I don't know if it counts as a major change, but I would expand the Town Hall Meeting to the entire office."

"Have you gotten a good response to those meetings?" Hannah asked.

"Incredible response," Aaron answered. "They ask great questions. In fact, sometimes Seth and I don't even know the answers. There's just a great dialogue about the vision of the department in these meetings, and I think the entire department could benefit if we had one big Town Hall Meeting."

"Done," Hannah stated. "Announce the change next week when you're in control, but wait until I get back to have the meeting. I want to participate and see how it goes. It may work well for 50 people, but it may be too big with 100. But I'm willing to try, and I think it would mean a lot if it came from you when you're in charge."

As they ate dinner and solved the problems of the world, Seth was wondering what change he would make. The opportunity to share his ideas would come soon enough.

A LESSON FOR THE TEACHER

When Hannah had told her management team she'd let them know when it was time to discuss Jill's replacement, Seth figured they would get plenty of notice. As it turned out, they got about an hour.

"I appreciate you making the time for this meeting," Hannah started. "I had hoped we would have more time to discuss Jill's replacement, but I just got word of a manager in my old department who's looking to move to this area. She would be a great asset to this team."

"Is this meeting to discuss how we go about replacing Jill," Carmen asked, "or is it just to approve whoever you think we should have?"

"I'm sure some of you have thoughts on her replacement, but if we wait too long, this person is not going to be available and . . ."

"Hey, wait a minute," Carmen interrupted. "Doesn't this go against what you've been teaching us in Engaged Leadership? This is a major change for our management team, and you've done nothing to prepare us for the change. In fact, you're just cramming it down our throats. And you certainly haven't empowered any of us in the process, since you went out and found your own person."

Everyone sat silently. Seth was shocked that Carmen would speak to her boss that way. Seth was even more shocked that what she said about Hannah was right.

After an extended period of silence, Hannah finally spoke up. "At least I know you were listening in all those quarterly meetings," Hannah said as she looked directly at Carmen. "I owe you and the entire team an apology. In my haste to get the person I thought would be right for the job, I didn't practice what I preach. I'm sorry for that."

After another moment of awkward silence, Aaron jumped in. "I can't believe it. It's taken a year, but we finally determined Hannah is human."

When everyone laughed at Aaron's comment, Seth could feel the tension leave the room.

"I am human, Aaron," Hannah said, "and I will make mistakes. I do my best to not make many of them, but they'll happen. I hold you accountable to building this culture, and I expect you to hold me accountable."

Seth realized the teacher had just become the student.

JILL'S REPLACEMENT

"Let's try this again," Hannah smiled. "As you all know, Jill has decided to leave the ranks of management to return to her roots as a call center rep. Her departure will leave a vacancy as of the beginning of next year. This meeting is to discuss how we proceed in filling Jill's position."

Everyone smiled at Hannah's formal approach.

"As a member of this management team, your input is critical. Whoever fills her position is going to be a part of this team and will be helping us maintain the culture of employee engagement we've worked so hard to build. Not only is it important this person be able to help us maintain the culture, it is imperative we use this opportunity to identify and position the appropriate talent for our needs at this time. Based on my background and experience in another department at Halifax, I have someone in mind for that position. However, before I share my thoughts, I'm interested to hear what you have to say."

As expected, Carmen jumped right in. "I have someone in mind for the position."

"Who do you have in mind?" Hannah asked.

"Kris Archer."

"Why Kris?" Hannah asked.

"Because she's earned a promotion. She's been here almost eighteen years now, and she's been overlooked every time a management position comes open. She's one of our best call center reps, and she deserves the recognition."

Aaron could never pass on an opportunity to take a jab at Carmen. "You didn't list one single reason why I should seriously consider Kris Archer for Jill's position. I know Kris. She's a wonderful person, but I don't think she's the right person for this job."

Before anyone else could say a word, Jill jumped in. "I agree with Aaron. If we promote her for the reasons you just gave, you'll make the same mistake with her that you made with me. If you think she has the skills and knowledge to be a great manager, promote her. If you think she has the right attitude that can help her along until the skills and knowledge catch up, promote her. But don't take one of our most engaged and effective reps and turn her into one of our most disengaged and ineffective managers just because you think it's her turn."

Jill made some great points, and Hannah knew it. "Perhaps we are getting the cart before the horse on this issue," she said. "We're trying to take a person and make her fit the job. Perhaps we should step back and identify what kind of person we're looking for, and then decide if either candidate we're considering is a good fit."

Everyone around the table nodded, including Carmen. For the next few hours, they made a list of the characteristics for the ideal manager, and identified the personal values the person would need to have. Ultimately, they decided skills weren't nearly as important as attitude. Hannah said she could teach the skills, but she couldn't teach the attitude. The person would need to bring the right attitude to the table.

After a lengthy discussion, the team decided that neither candidate was the right person to move into Jill's position. The next day they began a search for a new manager.

THANKSGIVING DINNER

Seth had been looking forward to November. He certainly enjoyed the cooler days, but it was more than the weather. When he looked back on the year, he was grateful for so many things that had happened over the past months. Personally, it was a fun year. He moved to a new town and met some new friends. Professionally, it was a learning year. He got to learn every single day from a wonderful boss, and got to work with some great employees. It was all good.

Seth was leaving the day before Thanksgiving to head home to be with his family. He loved Thanksgiving because it was an opportunity to get together with family and share those things for which he was thankful. It seemed appropriate to do the same with his new family at work.

He had never cooked a turkey before, and he certainly hadn't made all the other things that went along with a complete Thanksgiving dinner. But he made his team a deal. If they provided all the side dishes, he would bring the turkey.

Seth had no idea so much work went into cooking a turkey. It seemed like every few minutes he was back in the kitchen basting that giant bird. But when he walked into the conference room with it on a platter, all his efforts were worth it.

Every possible side dish was on the table that day. It was a great meal. And after the food was gone, they sat around and shared the things for which they were thankful. Seth enjoyed the food and certainly enjoyed the conversation. However, his favorite part of the afternoon was comparing the team of employees who had filed into that same conference room eleven months earlier as though they were attending a funeral to the team of employees who today laughed together and enjoyed each other's company.

Seth hoped he helped Hannah create a culture in that office. But even if he hadn't, he could leave knowing he helped create a family of friends. If nothing else, he was thankful for that.

ONE LAST VISIT TO LA CANTINA

The November results hadn't come out yet when Seth and Hannah agreed to meet at La Cantina. Quite frankly, neither of them was too concerned at that point, not because they didn't care if they were bad, but because they knew they would be good.

Seth spent a lot of time that year worried about how he ranked with his peers. His competitive nature provided the drive that made him want to win, and his commitment to Hannah to turn his team around was always at the back of his mind.

But Hannah always said that once employees were engaged and wanted to be a part of the team, there would be less need to worry about results. Seth figured they had gotten to that point as they met at La Cantina that December evening.

"I remember how I felt when you walked into the conference room in January and told us about the Employee Engagement Survey," Seth said. "I recall not caring what anyone said in that survey because it wouldn't be about me, but I was extremely worried what the following December survey would show. I never would have thought it wouldn't be a concern twelve months later."

"You were worried about the December survey?" Hannah laughed.

"Scared to death. I had no idea what I was doing, and prayed your lessons on Engaged Leadership would work. At that point, I had no idea if my employees would even respond to me."

"You did a good job of hiding it," Hannah said.

"When are they doing the survey?"

"Next week. They have it scheduled before most employees start taking off for the holiday," Hannah replied.

"I think they should hand it out at the company Christmas party. That should help us out."

"I haven't told the other managers this news yet because it isn't official, and I know how the rumor mill works," Hannah said. "I got a call from

Amanda Suttle. She wants to know if I'd be willing to run a region. She interviewed me when I was in New Jersey and wants me to come up for a job visit after the beginning of the year."

"A promotion?"

"Oh, yeah. I would be peers with my boss, Mr. Harrison," Hannah smiled.

Seth always wondered why Hannah stayed at Halifax. She could easily run her own company, and he knew she wouldn't be around long if someone didn't recognize her talents and promote her to the next level.

"If you get promoted, I'm going to need you to move your things out of the office as soon as possible. I want plenty of time to get settled!"

"Very funny," Hannah laughed. "I don't think the company plans to keep you here much longer. Your one-year assignment will be up soon, and you'll be off to conquer the world. But I have to say, I think this office would do great things if you were the boss."

"I appreciate that. I'm sure Carmen will do a great job leading this department into the future," Seth replied sarcastically.

"Did I forget to mention that part of your one-year assignment is you're required to take Carmen with you wherever you go for your next job?" Hannah laughed.

"The twelfth lesson in Engaged Leadership is establishing a strategy to maintain success, so I'm sure you've been thinking about your replacement."

"I haven't been thinking about my replacement," Hannah said. "I've been planning for my replacement since the day I got here."

"Aaron?"

"I suppose I could have gone outside the department to find someone," Hannah replied, "and I certainly would have if there wasn't an option here.

But Aaron showed promise from the very beginning. He just needed some development. He needed the opportunity to get some victories under his belt to build his confidence. He's responded well, and I think he's ready."

"Does he know?"

"He knows I'm grooming him for a promotion some day, but he doesn't know I'm being considered for another job. I don't want to get his hopes up if it falls through."

After they finished their dinner, they paid the check and headed out the door. Seth had a feeling that this might have been his last time with Hannah at La Cantina.

THE ANNOUNCEMENT

Seth had never seen Carmen smile. At one point he saw what appeared to be a grin when her team edged out his team on a monthly report. A grin was as good as it got.

That all changed when the announcement was made. Hannah brought the management team into the conference room on a Friday afternoon in January to make the announcement that Seth had been given a new assignment in a different city. He would finish out the month and report to his new job the first of February. Carmen didn't grin when she heard the news. She smiled from ear to ear.

Before he left that month, Seth had the honor of presenting Mattie with a plaque for one year of perfect attendance. He also got to see the results of the Employee Engagement Survey. Needless to say, they had a considerable improvement and beat the Austin office. Surprisingly, everyone got their bonuses, including Carmen.

Prior to his departure, he had one last piece of business to handle. While he didn't enjoy this particular task, he had learned that some people never make the transition to a new culture. Larry Marcus had not, and Seth provided him the opportunity to pursue a new career outside Halifax.

It turned out that leaving would be much harder for Seth than he thought it would be. When he had arrived at this job, he saw it as a stepping-stone to the next job. He had never expected to learn as much as he did, and he certainly hadn't expected to make the friends he made.

One part of him was ready to go. He made a difference with this team, and he was ready to take on the next challenge. This opportunity provided him so many skills that he would be much more prepared for the next assignment. He was prepared to keep his promise to Amanda and pass along the development.

But another part of Seth was sad to leave. He knew he made a difference while changing the culture, but he knew there would always be a "Carmen" to shift the team back to the old culture. In fact, he could see it in their eyes at his going-away party.

Seth learned a lesson about culture on the way to that office a year earlier, and he learned a lesson on the way out. When managers come and go, it's imperative to change the culture if you want it to survive long after you're gone. Seth looked back and realized what he helped Hannah create really was a culture. These weren't just activities or motivational tactics. This was a culture. It was a way of life for these employees.

Seth didn't get to pick his successor. In fact, he learned months later that a replacement was not hired. The employees on his team were divided up among the remaining three managers. He thought about them often, and hoped that a little part of the culture he helped create may have rubbed off on the managers who took on his team members. Whether it did or not, Seth knew he had made an impact because he helped these "misfits" experience the feeling of success. He made them feel appreciated. He let them know they were winners.

Seth also learned it's hard to change a culture in a year. He learned it's hard, but not impossible.

Epilogue
One Year Later

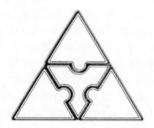

FINAL DESCENT

Seth was reclining comfortably when he felt the tap on his shoulder. He opened his eyes and saw the flight attendant smiling down at him. He sat up and removed the headset from his ears.

"We're on our final descent into Newark, Mr. Owen," she said politely. "I need you to raise your seatback and finish your drink. We'll be landing soon."

"Sorry about that," Seth responded as he turned off his iPad and closed the cover. "I didn't hear the announcement. These noise-canceling headsets work *really* well."

He finished his drink and handed the empty glass to the flight attendant. As she walked away, Seth pulled out his cell phone so he could send a text the moment the plane landed. This was a text he had been looking forward to sending for a year.

ON THE GROUND

Aaron was sitting in the baggage claim area when he got the text: *On the ground!* He had arrived into the Newark airport an hour earlier than Seth. Rather than taking a cab upon his own arrival, he agreed to wait for Seth so they could ride together. Although they had talked frequently on the telephone and shared numerous e-mails, this was the first time they would see each other face-to-face in a year.

Seth and Aaron had worked together for only a year, but it was a life-changing year for them both. It was Seth's first year in the real working world, and Aaron's first year of being molded for greater opportunities. Under Hannah's guidance, they grew as leaders together, and in the process, created a friendship for life.

After his year in the field working in the call center, Seth transferred to the staff where he gained insights into the financial side of the business. Amanda Suttle knew the impact Seth had in his first year, and she wanted him to share those experiences with other call center leaders. After six short months, she made it possible for him to be promoted into human resources, giving him the opportunity to travel to call centers around the country sharing his story as a trainer on the topic of leadership.

Several months after Seth was gone, the promotion Hannah had spoken of for herself became a reality. She was promoted to run a region in the Pacific Northwest, and as she had planned, she promoted Aaron to fill her shoes. For nearly eight months now, Aaron had been running the call center just outside Austin. Hard work and development had paid off for them all.

Seth and Aaron were coming together in Newark for a leadership conference held by Halifax at the beginning of each year. They both were looking forward to the conference, but they were really looking forward to the opportunity to catch up throughout the week.

Seth was the first passenger to arrive in the baggage claim area. "First person off the plane," Aaron said as he walked toward Seth. "Must be nice riding in First Class."

"That's what happens when you travel several times a week for the past six months," Seth replied with a smile as he greeted his friend with a hug. "Free upgrades!"

After they'd gathered their bags, they jumped in a cab and were headed for the hotel.

GETTING SETTLED

Seth and Aaron headed to their rooms to get unpacked for the week. They agreed to meet downstairs in the lobby at 6 o'clock to go to dinner. Aaron assumed it would be the two of them. Unbeknownst to Aaron, Seth had made dinner reservations for three. As Seth was hanging out in his room, he received the text he had been waiting for all day: *On the ground! See you at 6 in the hotel lobby.* The reunion wouldn't be complete without the one who made it all happen— Hannah Jaxson.

THE REUNION

Seth hadn't seen Hannah since he left the call center a year ago, so he didn't know what to expect. People change, he thought. Some people gain weight. Some people color or cut their hair. He had no idea what to expect. But when the glass doors opened in the lobby, he had a flashback to that first day in the airport when they first met. Dressed in a dark blue suit, Hannah still carried herself with all the confidence in the world.

"My children have all grown up," Hannah said as she walked toward Seth and Aaron with open arms. "You found your way to the airport and got here all on your own!"

"Sort of," Aaron replied with a smile as he got a hug from his mentor. "I wasn't sure Seth could make it from the airport, so I waited an hour just to be sure."

"I'm guessing the globe-trotter could have gotten here all on his own," Hannah smiled as she turned toward Seth with a giant hug and a kiss on the cheek. "I'm looking forward to catching up over dinner. Let me get checked in and freshened up, and we'll get out of here."

"I've made dinner reservations for 7 o'clock right down the street," Seth replied. "We're in no hurry, so take your time. We'll be waiting in the bar."

DINNER

"All the great places to eat in Newark and you choose a Mexican food restaurant," Hannah laughed as they were seated by the hostess at Casa Rio.

"Our reunion would not be complete without a great margarita," Seth responded as he pulled out his chair. "I did my research, and this place claims to have the best."

"Well, it may not be La Cantina," Aaron chimed in, "but the ambiance is bringing back some great memories."

They put in an order for a round of margaritas, and warned the waitress they might be there a while. They had a lot of catching up to do.

"So, how's the big promotion treating you?" Seth asked Hannah.

"Good," she replied as she leaned back in her chair. "I have eight direct reports, all of which are running a call center. Some are better than others, but overall it's been fun."

"Tell us about your biggest challenge," Aaron asked.

Hannah thought for a moment. "The adjustments we've had to make throughout the recession have made it difficult to keep everyone engaged throughout the regions. We'll be closing one of the call centers in my region, and no one knows which it will be at this point. All eight of my direct reports are anxious."

"I would have thought all that anxiety would have made them more engaged," Aaron responded. "They have to know that Halifax won't cut the call center with the most engagement."

"I didn't say they weren't working hard," Hannah smiled, "but I'm not fooling myself into believing their hard work is a sign of engagement. I have no doubt the things I'm doing are building a culture of engagement, but I'm sure a certain part of their hard work is a sign of fear and anxiety at this point. Real engagement will ensure the productivity is there after the fear and anxiety are gone, so I'm working hard to keep them engaged despite the unknown. In the absence of engagement, maintaining good performance is a crapshoot after the fear and anxiety is gone, and I refuse to gamble by assuming their hard work is the result of pure engagement."

The waitress arrived with the margaritas as Hannah finished her point. She looked across the table at Aaron and asked, "So, let's talk about how you're settling in to your new role. Are you wishing you'd turned down the promotion yet?"

"Not a chance," Aaron replied. "I love it. Our region has been feeling the pinch of the recession. Unlike your region, we actually closed a call center two months ago, even after the company said it wouldn't happen."

"What's that done to the culture?" Seth asked. "You haven't undone all the hard work we put into that office, have you?"

"No, the culture is still good," Aaron responded. "In fact, we've actually enjoyed some benefits from the closing. When you left the call center, the decision was made to not replace you. But after we began getting some of the traffic from the closed call center, I was able to convince my boss to allow me to fill your old position. The company sent me one of the managers from the closed call center. So, now we're back to having four managers."

"So who are your managers now?" Hannah asked.

"I've got Lee Jeffries, the manager from the closed call center, and Miles Freeman, who got promoted to take Jill's place when she went back to being a call center rep. The corporate headquarters sent me a college recruit named

Ryan Kilpatrick to take my position when I got promoted. Good kid, just needs a lot of development. And, of course, our favorite person in the world, Carmen Fuentes."

"You didn't get rid of her," Seth laughed. "I thought for sure she would be gone the day you took over."

"It crossed my mind. After working with her for so long, and seeing the many efforts Hannah made to engage her, I realized she's in the wrong job. I'm not convinced there's not a seat for her somewhere on the Halifax bus."

"Have you found her another seat?" Hannah asked.

"I did. I worked with another call center manager in another city who agreed to take her. Believe it or not, Carmen agreed to the change. And just as we started the paperwork, the company put a freeze on relocation funds because of the recession. No one can relocate to another city until the company lifts the freeze."

"So other than finding a new home for our friend Carmen, what's your biggest leadership challenge?" Seth asked.

"The leadership challenges aren't much different than they were when you were there," Aaron answered. "I've been introducing the Engaged Leadership model to my management team, and it's been fun watching the concepts get applied in the call center. I guess my biggest concern at this point is a potential mass exodus of my best people when times get better. We have asked them to pick up a lot of slack with the closing of the call center, and I'm concerned it may be wearing them out."

"So what are you doing about it?" Hannah asked.

"Well, we're communicating more than ever. We're telling them good news as often as we can, and we're telling them bad news when it's something they need to know. Essentially, we're being as transparent as possible. We've learned to say thank you in every possible way. We've ensured they know the managers haven't gotten any raises or bonuses during the tough times. Any financial resources we get we use on them, not on us. And we try to keep their eye on the future by communicating a positive vision for the future."

Aaron paused long enough to take a sip of his margarita, and then looked toward Seth. "Well, globe-trotter, what about you?"

"My situation is a little different, I suppose," Seth started. "When I left the call center, I went to the staff and stared at financial reports for six months. I didn't have any direct reports to lead. Then when I moved over to human resources, I took on this training assignment. I still don't have any direct reports to lead."

"But you spend a lot of time in the field," Hannah replied.

"I do, and I get to see and hear a lot. Much of what I'm seeing and hearing is similar to what you are sharing. These are tough times. Even as we come out of the recession, it's not like previous recessions. I'm not convinced we'll ever return to where we were. I think we'll need to evolve if we're going to compete."

"Anything in particular stand out as an issue?" Hannah asked.

"Well, again, the concerns are the same just about everywhere I travel," Seth replied. "Perhaps the one thing that stands out to me the most is that not one single issue we're facing as an organization can't be dealt with by providing strong leadership.

I see some leaders getting worried and retreating to old management styles. They aren't communicating, and they're watching out for themselves. Nothing we're facing in this company can't be overcome if we simply keep our focus on building a culture of employee engagement."

"Well, well, well," Hannah said with a smile. "I can't tell you how satisfying it is to see how far you've both come in a year. Our company will do well if more managers saw the significance of strong leadership to get us through any financial downturn. I'm proud of you both."

"We have you to thank," Aaron responded. "Good leadership starts at the top. You set a great example."

"There will be plenty more great examples to follow over the next few days at this leadership conference," she replied. "Let's make a deal. Let's meet back here on the last night of the conference to share the specific action items we've gained from this experience. From there, we'll determine the best ways to hold each other accountable for making progress over the next year."

"It's a deal," Seth responded. "But for now, let's eat."

For the next two hours, they got lost in conversation catching up on their personal lives. Three colleagues dedicated to being better leaders. Three colleagues dedicated to being better friends.

The Application of Engaged Leadership

Years ago I was scheduled to speak at a management conference for a large corporation. Prior to the event, I spent some time with the leader of the organization, explaining my plans for the talk, which was to be about engaging the disengaged employees in his company. I'll call him Greg.

"Why should we spend time with the lazy, unmotivated employees?" Greg asked. "I want you to teach my management team how to make their good people better! I'm getting rid of the lousy ones this year."

First of all, I'm a big believer in making good people better. Not only does it improve their performance, but it makes them feel appreciated and helps us retain the people we should be trying to retain. While there was nothing wrong with Greg's focus on his best employees, I needed to convince him of the importance of focusing on employee engagement.

After we spent some time together, I was able to persuade Greg that engaging the disengaged is an important way to make his good people better. Good people get worn out when they feel they're surrounded by employees who aren't dedicated to the organization.

Second, I was concerned with his comment about lazy, unmotivated employees. In his mind, anyone who wasn't one of the "good" employees he wanted to make better fell into the category of "lazy and unmotivated." Even after a significant amount of time discussing the importance of working on his disengaged employees, Greg still couldn't see the value in spending time with those disengaged employees. I was going to have to take a chance.

Many professional speakers will tell a client what he or she wants to hear, knowing they'll get glowing reviews and the opportunity to return in the future. I suppose there may have been a year or two early in my career when I did the same. I've learned over the years that it's not my job to tell a client what he wants to hear, but to tell the client what he needs to hear. This was one of those times.

"Greg," I asked, "if you have lazy, unmotivated employees, how do you suppose they got that way?"

He thought for a moment. "I don't know," he responded. "I guess they showed up that way."

After a brief chuckle, I replied, "Greg, if they showed up lazy and unmotivated, you do not have a management problem. You have a hiring problem. I'm not convinced you're hiring lazy, unmotivated employees. In fact, I bet they were enthusiastic and engaged when they first got here. Your management team caused them to become disengaged, and you have the responsibility to fix the problem. I can show you how to build a culture to overcome the employee disengagement that's holding you back."

Greg wasn't the first client to not understand disengaged employees, and will likely not be the last. The problem with his view of the workforce was that he divided his workers into two groups. He thought he had good employees and bad employees. Gallup's research mentioned throughout this book accurately describes *three* groups—the 29 percent at the top who are engaged, the 54 percent in the middle who are disengaged, and the 17 percent at the bottom who are actively disengaged. After explaining this to Greg, he admitted he lumped the middle 54 percent in with the 17 percent at the bottom.

This brings me to the third concern I had with Greg's initial comment. He said he planned to get rid of the "lousy ones" this year. There are certainly times when termination is the only remaining option for an employee, and I believe we should act quickly and decisively when we've come to that conclusion. However, I have seen that an all-too-common approach is to focus on the bad employees. "We need to get rid of these bad apples." "We need to put these people on a Performance Improvement Plan." "It's time to cut loose the negative characters."

I'm aware of the myriad of legal issues that must be maneuvered to terminate an employee, and strongly encourage anyone who has chosen that route to follow the law and the steps that must be taken. However, I don't believe eliminating the bottom 17 percent is effective as a strategy to improve an organization, and I have encountered many leaders who spend the majority of their time dealing with these actively disengaged employees.

I believe the biggest opportunity lies with the 54 percent of disengaged employees. Again, these aren't bad people. They simply see their work as just a job. In many cases, they have no idea how they contribute to the bigger picture. We all love being around the 29 percent who are engaged employees, and we should be doing everything possible to recognize their efforts and help improve their performance. However, our future success lies in our ability to engage the disengaged employee.

The issue of employee disengagement is a real concern for most organizations. While some people, like Greg, dismiss the problem as laziness or a lack of motivation on the part of the employee, the opportunity to overcome employee disengagement lies within the control of leadership. In fact, if you have disengaged employees, it's because you have disengaged leadership.

The solution is simple. Anyone in a position of leading employees has a responsibility to provide three aspects of leadership. As illustrated in the fable, the three aspects of Engaged Leadership are:

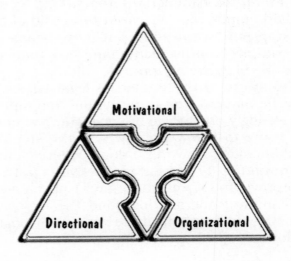

I have been introducing the concept of Engaged Leadership as a trainer, consultant, and professional speaker for many years now. What I have found is that many participants attempt to place employees within one of these three categories. Those at the top of the organization are expected to set the vision as Directional leaders. Those in middle management are expected to inspire the team to want to pursue the vision as Motivational leaders. And those on the front line are expected to develop the team as Organizational leaders. While that may seem natural, the concept behind Engaged Leadership requires that all leaders focus on all three aspects of leadership.

Also, the key to success with Engaged Leadership is not in understanding the concepts. In fact, the concepts of Engaged Leadership are not difficult, and are based on some universal, common-sense ideas in business today. The key to success with Engaged Leadership is in the application of the ideas.

In the fable, Hannah shared four lessons each in Directional, Motivational, and Organizational Leadership. To encourage you to put the concepts in this book to use within your organization, I am going to offer these lessons as challenges within the three areas of Engaged Leadership. Furthermore, I will offer some specific action items along with each challenge.

Let's get started with Directional Leadership.

Directional
Leadership

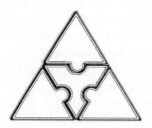

Some people are wonderful with details. They can take an incredible vision, break it down into bite-sized pieces, and identify a laundry list of tasks to be completed in order to realize the vision. I do everything I can to surround myself with these people, because I am not one of them.

I've had some moments of analysis paralysis where I consumed every detail of a project. But for the most part, I'm more a big-picture guy. I leave the details to someone else.

I've worked for companies of different sizes. I've worked as a front-line manager for a huge company, where the vision was decided at levels far beyond mine. I've worked as an executive for a midsized company, where the vision was decided by the chairman of the board. And I've worked as the principal of a consulting firm small enough to fit into your living room, where I was an integral part of creating the vision.

While each scenario was different, one aspect remained the same in each organization. The people responsible for carrying out the vision wanted to know what the vision was. They wanted to know how what they accomplished in their job contributed to the overall direction of the company. They wanted to be a part of something big.

This is the start of a wonderful thing. A vision has been created by those with the responsibility for setting the direction of the company. The employees responsible for carrying it out are anxious to know what it is, and how they can contribute to making it happen. Then somewhere between the development of the strategy and its implementation, something happens. Management doesn't pass the information along to the very people who can help the company realize the vision.

According to a survey by Right Management Consultants, a career transition and organizational consulting firm, about two-thirds of employees do not know or understand their employer's business strategy. How can we ever expect a team of employees to help us realize a vision when they don't even know or understand what that vision is?

Of the organizations responding to the survey, 28 percent limit such communication to only their leadership teams, 24 percent have not yet communicated the vision to all employees, and 15 percent are uncertain of the best way to do it.

Procrastination is pretty common, so I can understand the 24 percent that have not gotten around to communicating the vision, although I would remind them that an uninformed employee is a disengaged employee. I can even cut some slack for the 15 percent who just haven't figured out the best way to communicate the vision, but I would strongly encourage them to get it figured out.

The percentage in this survey that baffles me is the 28 percent that limit the communication of the business strategy to only their leadership teams, as though they are the only ones worthy of knowing the vision. And you've seen the scenario: The strategy is shared with a handful of key employees who are expected to use their genius to make it all happen. They scurry around working fourteen-hour days, and never let anyone in on the deal.

Whether you're creating a new vision or mission from scratch, or you're tweaking an existing vision or mission because of changing times, you have a responsibility to share it with the people who can help you realize the vision. Not just the people at the top. Not just the managers. Every single employee in the organization should know what it is, and how their work contributes to it. You do a disservice to yourself, your company, and your employees when you assume lower-level employees don't care about the business strategy of the organization.

The method you use to communicate the strategy will vary depending on the size of your organization. Some companies choose to hold Town Hall Meetings. Some engrave it on a plaque and hang it in the lobby or laminate cards for employees to carry around in their wallet. Pick a method that's appropriate for your organization. But once you've communicated the vision of the organization to every single person whose efforts contribute to the realization of that vision, the real work begins. Perhaps the most important thing you can do is build a consensus for the vision.

For those leaders who took part in creating the company's vision, buy-in is not too difficult. But for the vast number of employees who were not part of the planning process, buy-in may be hard. It's not that employees don't want to follow the direction. Quite often they just don't get it because they weren't a part of the process to develop the direction, and there wasn't a concentrated effort to help them get it. Directional Leadership is important because it provides the concentrated effort to build a consensus for the vision.

I know what some of you may be thinking: "We couldn't even get everyone on the leadership team to agree with the plan. How in the world are we going to get every employee in the company to agree with the plan?"

Building consensus is not about getting everyone to agree *with* the strategy. Building consensus is about getting everyone to agree *to* the strategy.

In the ideal world, employees at all levels would be involved in the development of the mission and vision of the organization, and everyone would agree with the direction. There is perhaps no better way to build consensus than to have buy-in from employees at all levels. Not only do you create buy-in of the vision, you let employees see how their work contributes to the vision.

But things don't always work that way in the real world. In the real world, the leadership of the organization creates the mission and vision, and the employees are expected to follow it. By instructing people to follow the vision rather than building consensus, we produce mediocrity at best. Quite simply, employees will show up to work and perform the function instead of pursuing the vision.

By meeting the four challenges as outlined in this section of Directional Leadership, leaders can increase the interest of employees by building consensus. Although increasing the interest of employees won't create employee engagement, it will start the process of moving them toward engagement.

CHALLENGE ONE: RECRUIT SUPPORT FROM THE TOP 29 PERCENT

According to the study by the Gallup Organization referenced in the Introduction, 29 percent of employees are engaged. These are the employees who are excited to be on the team. While you are off putting out fires and running the day-to-day operations of the business, these dedicated and productive employees are getting the work done.

The support of this group is critical in any organization. Once they're committed to the vision, you know they'll give 100 percent of their effort to help make it happen. The success of any plan needs a group whose only gear is "full steam ahead" once they've been convinced the direction is the right one.

Although the work these employees do is significant to helping the organization realize the vision, perhaps the more important contribution is one of influence. You see, the 54 percent of disengaged employees are looking for direction. In any organization, they get it from either the 29 percent of people who buy in to the vision, or they get it from the 17 percent of actively disengaged people who exist on this earth for the sole purpose of blocking your vision. Although you may have significant influence as the leader of your organization, the likelihood of the disengaged employee embracing your vision increases significantly when their peers support your vision. Your engaged employees are a direct link to the 54 percent of disengaged employees.

To get you started, here are some recommended action items to help you recruit support from the top 29 percent:

- *Identify your top 29 percent.* The first step is to identify your engaged employees. Sit down and create a list. Pinpoint the people you believe can influence their peers.
- *Bring them together as a group.* Once you've identified your top 29 percent, present your plan to them as a group before you attempt to introduce the vision to the entire organization. You can't assume they'll support the plan. You have to convince them the vision is a good one.
- *Solicit their input into the vision.* Depending on the size of your organization, you may never get 100 percent of your employees to provide input into the vision. But you could get input from your top 29 percent. If you allow this group to provide input, it will do three things. One, these employees wouldn't just be supporting *your* plan to the 54 percent of disengaged employees. In their minds, they'd be supporting *their* plan to the 54 percent of disengaged employees. Second, your disengaged employees would give more credibility to the vision if they knew it was created by some of their own. And third, because they are in the trenches every day, they may be able to tell you if something won't work.

- *Ask them to recruit the other 54 percent.* As mentioned before, your top 29 percent is the direct link to your disengaged employees. If your top 29 percent is respected by their peers, they just may have a better chance of building consensus for the vision than anyone in management.

The responsibility for building consensus lies with the leadership of the organization. Smart leaders know how to leverage the resources around them to help build the organization. The 29 percent of engaged employees is a tremendous resource for building consensus.

CHALLENGE TWO: PREPARE THE ORGANIZATION FOR CHANGE

Few organizations will be able to conduct "business as usual" after they emerge from the recession. As organizations find their new "normal," a new or adjusted vision will bring change, and most employees will not readily accept it. That's not surprising. In fact, it's simply not normal to eagerly accept change. If we do, it's probably because we were a part of the initial discussion and can see the benefit of the change, or it was our idea in the first place. Either way, we've seen the future with the change in place, and we're willing to move in that direction.

For the majority in your organization, however, the benefit of the change may not be so obvious. Each employee has his or her own way of dealing with change. In fact, there are three different ways a disengaged employee will react to change: (1) There are those who will ignore it, and just keep doing what they were doing before.

(2) There are those who will fight it because they don't buy into the reasons for the change, or it is their sole mission in life to keep everything the same. (3) There are those who will react to it, either positively or negatively. For most disengaged employees, the reaction is usually negative.

Too often as leaders we just introduce change and assume our employees will accept whatever change we tell them to accept. After all, we're paying them to do a job. As Directional leaders, we have a responsibility to prepare the organization for change.

To get you started, here are some recommended action items to help you prepare the organization for change:

- *Agree on unity with your leadership team.* Many employees will react to a change based on the way their manager reacts to the change. I once worked for a boss who introduced a change in departmental policy with the following announcement. "As you know, the department has been considering this change. Although I don't agree with it, the decision has been made. Quite frankly, I think it's stupid, and I don't want to do it, but it seems we don't have a choice." How many of us on that team do you think supported the change? Not many. As a leader, you have a responsibility to stand up and fight for whatever you know to be right when you're with your leadership team. But when the decision is made, regardless of what position you took prior to the change, you have a responsibility to stand behind it 100 percent (provided the change is not illegal or immoral). If you don't, then you've shown your employees that the leadership team can't even agree to the change. The first step toward preparing your team for change is to have a leadership team on the same page.

- *Give the reason for the change.* A person doesn't have to agree with a change to accept it. Remember, you don't have to get everyone to agree *with* the change. You just have to get them to agree *to* the change. And most reasonable employees will accept it if it makes sense, even if they don't particularly like it.
- *Tell employees how the change will affect them.* Somewhere in the back of employees' minds they may be wondering how a change will affect the organization. But the only thing employees really want to know is how the change is going to affect *them.* Many employees have experienced emotional and psychological trauma as they've seen organizations downsize throughout the recession. Change will make them nervous, since it may require them to get out of their comfort zone. It will be imperative you tell them how the change will affect them. Tell them up front, and there's a better chance they will accept the change.
- *Use data to tell the story.* The world is full of left-brained, detail people. When they hear someone in leadership say, "I think building a new store in this area is important to the company," it means very little to them. But if they hear, "I think building a new store in this area is important to the company because the most recent survey of this area indicates a 74 percent growth in population in the next five years. By purchasing the land and building a new store now, we project an increase of

250 employees to our workforce, and profits of more than ten million dollars in the fifth year." Numbers can be powerful. In fact, numbers drive many of the changes our companies make. If they help build consensus of the vision, use them to tell your story.

- *Introduce the change as improvement, not change.* Nearly all change is implemented because someone believes it will lead to something better. I have heard many people say, "Oh no, not more change!" but I've never heard anyone say, "Oh no, not more improvement!" It may be a simple concept, but it helps employees deal with change.

- *Celebrate the past and the future.* The change you are introducing may be the best idea in the world. But if people feel the new way is a rejection of their old way, most will object to the change. Celebrate the successes of the past. If you let employees know you move forward on the shoulders of the people who succeeded in the past, you have a better chance of getting them to accept the change.

Most organizations that stay the same get left behind—particularly those that refuse to reinvent themselves on the other side of the recession. To move forward, change is required. Finding a way to help employees through the change is a key to building consensus toward the vision.

CHALLENGE THREE: LET THEM KNOW HOW THEY CONTRIBUTE

You can develop a wonderful vision to take your organization to the next level, but if your employees don't know what they're supposed to do to help realize the vision, the vision won't matter. Although communicating the vision is essential, ensuring each and every employee knows what he or she is expected to do to contribute is vital to your success. Too often we assume people know what to do, and then get frustrated when they don't perform well because they don't know what's expected of them.

My experience has shown me that some people are quite good at communicating expectations. The parent who looks at a child and says, "Get upstairs and get your homework done!" The supervisor who looks at an employee and says, "I expect you to start showing up on time!" The wife who looks at her husband and says, "You need to pick up the dry cleaning on your way home from work." In these scenarios, the leader is clearly communicating the expectation.

The missing element in all three examples is a consequence. Every decision we make in life is driven by an expectation and a consequence. We get up and go to work because we don't like the consequence of losing our job and the income that comes with our employment. We put gas in our car because we don't want to be stranded on the side of the road. We pay our utility bill because we don't want our electricity turned off. I could go on and on.

In his book *Bringing Out the Best in People* (McGraw-Hill, 1999), Aubrey C. Daniels supports this belief with the theory that every behavior has a consequence, and that the consequence that follows a certain behavior will significantly affect whether or not a person will repeat this behavior. He goes on to show the impact of positive versus negative consequences, future versus immediate consequences, and certain versus uncertain consequences. His observations on the idea of expectations and consequences are right on target.

If we know behavior is directed by its consequence, then we have a responsibility to communicate the consequence up front. If we wait until the expectation is not met to decide the consequence, then we didn't give the consequence an opportunity to drive behavior. At that point, the consequence is merely a punishment.

Imagine the mother who tells her son to be home at 10 o'clock. When the boy shows up at 11 o'clock, she grounds him for a week. When he screams, "That's not fair!" he's right. Fair would be telling him he has to be home at 10, and if he's late, he'll be grounded for a week. By knowing the consequence, the young man has an opportunity to decide his own fate.

Some people have told me they won't set a consequence because they don't want to be seen as the bad guy when they have to enforce the consequence. First of all, if you're not setting consequences with employees because you don't want to be seen as the bad guy, find another profession. Management is not for you. Second, enforcing a consequence does not make you a bad guy. Making up a consequence after the expectation is not met makes you a bad guy.

To get you started, here are some recommended action items to help you be extremely clear about what you want:

- *Assess how well you've communicated expectations.* Stop right now and determine if you've clearly communicated expectations to the employees in your organization. Do they know exactly what they need to do to

help your company realize its vision? Don't
assume they know. In fact, the easiest way to
complete this task is to ask your employees
for clarification of their responsibilities. You
may be surprised what you hear.

- *Let employees create the expectations
  through goal setting.* The vision should be
  translated into actionable goals. Let employees decide what those goals are. If their goals
  aren't big enough, deal with it then. Employees have a better chance of achieving the
  goals if they set them themselves.
- *Assess how well you've communicated consequences.* Once you've established you
  have done a good job communicating expectations and every employee knows what to do
  to contribute, ask yourself if consequences
  are in place that will drive the behavior you
  want. In fact, take a look at your biggest
  performance challenge today and decide if
  the absence of a consequence may be the
  cause of the poor performance.
- *Determine positive consequences that would
  drive behavior.* Although the word *consequence* has a negative connotation, not all
  consequences have to be negative. In fact, a
  negative consequence should be used only
  when an employee's performance has not
  been motivated by a positive consequence.
- *Ensure the consequence motivates the behavior.* My mother tells the story that she
  learned very early in my life that spanking
  me had very little effect. She was smart
  enough to notice that without my bicycle, I
  couldn't ride around the neighborhood with
  my friends. She learned that any time she set
  an expectation for me that she thought I

might not meet, she would set a consequence of losing the use of my bicycle for a
week. It never failed.

In the ideal world, a leader could communicate
expectations and everyone would run out and produce great results. In the real world, however,
where three-quarters of any organization is disengaged, a leader must communicate expectations
and consequences, and enforce the consequences.
Over time, when employees see they've determined
their own fate, a culture of employee engagement
will develop, and you'll find less need for negative
consequences.

CHALLENGE FOUR: CONSTANTLY COMMUNICATE PROGRESS

Whether you've developed a vision for the company from scratch or revisited existing ones to
ensure they still fit the company's direction, any
change in direction will bring a certain level of
fear from management and employees. Managers will often fear a loss of authority when
decision making is pushed down the organization. Employees will fear punishment if they've
been empowered to make decisions they've never
made before.

The level of fear felt by both sides depends on
how significant the changes are to the direction of
the organization. If there have been substantial
changes, employees and management will lean
toward going back to the old way of doing things.
In the absence of strong leadership and information informing them of the team's progress,
employees will inevitably yearn for the old way

of doing things and gradually creep back in that direction.

To ensure both management and employees get past those initial fears and stay on task, constant communication regarding progress is critical. In the previous challenge we looked at the importance of letting employees know how they contribute. Once an employee knows how his work contributes to the vision, he must know if the organization and the work he's doing is making progress.

To get you started, here are some recommended action items to help you communicate progress:

- *Create a method to share information regularly.* To build consensus, the vision of the organization must be put in front of the employees on a regular basis. Also, the vision must be communicated in different formats. Create an internal newsletter, create a blog, hang it on the wall. Different methods work for different companies. Just get in front of the team regularly.
- *Let employees know where they stand.* Not only do employees need to know what progress the company is making, they need to know how their work is contributing. Tell them how they're doing. Don't procrastinate in giving good or bad feedback. Not just annual reviews. Give them regular updates.
- *Host a quarterly vision review meeting.* In a Town Hall format, host a meeting where all employees have the opportunity to provide feedback on the vision. Allow for input

into changes in the vision. Make it a place where open critique is encouraged. Show that you are willing, and able, to defend your position.

We all tend to get off task in a world where we spend so much time putting out fires. If you want the message to stick, you must find ways to constantly communicate progress.

Motivational Leadership

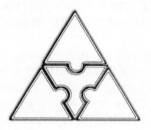

The vision of the organization has been established. You've encouraged your engaged employees to influence those who are disengaged. Employees know how they contribute to the success of the organization and are driven by consequences that will inspire them to be successful. You've prepared them for the improvements that will come as a result of your enhanced vision, and you're keeping them informed of their progress. A culture of employee engagement is developing.

As this culture takes shape, some employees will choose to leave. They may not like the new direction, there may be too much change, or their values simply don't work with the new vision. It's expected some employees will leave for those reasons, as well as other legitimate reasons. Some leave for more money, while some simply move away. Some choose to leave the workforce to raise children, while some want to follow their entrepreneurial inclinations.

These are all acceptable reasons to lose an employee. But the vast majority of employees don't leave for those reasons. In fact, the vast majority don't leave companies. They leave bosses. They were unhappy with how they were treated, or they didn't feel their work was appreciated. In a nutshell, they left because they weren't motivated to stay.

Seldom will an employee say they're leaving because of a lack of motivation. Any time a friend or colleague changes jobs, I always ask what caused them to leave. Most often it's because they had a boss who focused only on what they did wrong instead of inspiring them by focusing on what they did right. They left because they felt the needs of the business always came first, and their needs were overlooked.

When company leaders examine who they're losing, it's usually their engaged employees. "How can you leave?" they ask. "You're the only one I can depend on around here." Sadly, engaged employees are leaving because they were the only ones management could depend on, and they were left alone. Sometimes we spend so much time trying to engage the disengaged that we forget to take care of the ones taking care of the organization.

Whether we've lost our best employees because they felt ignored, or we've lost our disengaged employees because they never felt they were a part of the bigger picture, the result is the same. Turnover. And turnover is costly to any business. Some expenses associated with replacing employees are obvious. Advertisements must be run in local newspapers, and temporary employees may need to be hired to cover the work until a new employee is hired. In some cases, uniforms must be purchased, and investments in new equipment must be made.

If the cost of turnover was limited to the obvious expenses, then turnover could be measured and managed in almost any business. However, the most negative impact of turnover is found in the hidden costs—lost productivity of peers, the learning curve of a replacement, lower morale of remaining employees due to added workload, loss of organizational knowledge, client issues due to turnover, and so on. Some research indicates the cost of replacing an employee can be anywhere between one and three times the lost employee's annual salary.

Management has a right to expect employees to come to the table with a certain level of motivation, and quite often they do. However, keep in mind that an employee's success will be based on four things: skills, knowledge, resource, and motivation. Some employees leave an organization because the company fails to train employees so the proper skills can be attained. Some employees leave because communication from management is so poor the employee doesn't have the knowledge to be successful. And sometimes employees leave a company because management refuses to invest the resources to be successful. But by far the most common reason for an employee leaving is motivation.

By meeting the four challenges as outlined in this Motivational Leadership section, leaders can begin to build a culture of motivation to overcome employee disengagement.

CHALLENGE FIVE: LEAD WITH POSITIVE MOTIVATION

I was standing to the left of the stage in a very large ballroom preparing to speak to a group of 300 construction supervisors. I was delivering a speech titled "Motivational Leadership: The Inspirational Side of Engaged Leadership." The CEO of the company walked on stage to give the introduction.

"Alright, alright. Sit down, shut up, and listen," he started. "I have two things to say. One, I better not see anyone fall asleep in my meeting. Between the hotel charges, the food bill, and all the travel expenses, I paid a bunch of money for you all to be here. If I catch one of you sleeping in my meeting, you're fired. Second, you need to pay attention because we've paid this guy to come in here and help us motivate the troops." He then turned to me and said, "And you better do a good job." He turned back to the audience and said, "Please help me welcome Cliff Swindell."

I have had the pleasure of speaking to several hundred audiences and have enjoyed many different introductions. Never in my life had I experienced an introduction quite like that one. It was awful on so many levels, the least of which was that he couldn't even get my name right.

The evening before the speech I had the opportunity to spend some time with this CEO and some of his leadership team. It was apparent to me from the beginning of the evening that he was feared by his leadership team. He had a very strong personality, to which I am certain he attributes his success as a leader.

As a student of human behavior and leadership in particular, I was analyzing his leadership style throughout dinner. Based on our conversation, it was clear that he saw himself as a visionary leader. In a very common approach to leadership, he had the vision, communicated it to his team, and directed them to pursue it.

At no point did I ever get the impression he believed he needed to inspire anyone to pursue the vision. His method of motivation was intimidation, and he expected everyone to perform or they could find their way to the door. What an exciting place to work!

I'm not denying the considerable power in negative motivation and management by intimidation. In fact, there's no need to look very far to see organizations built on foundations of negative motivation. Fear is a strong motivating factor. I simply believe that negative motivation and management by intimidation will get people to do things for the wrong reason. Although it will help realize short-term results, it will do nothing to create engaged employees. In fact, it will do just the opposite.

Some people enjoy focusing on negative motivation. In fact, we've probably all worked for someone who thrived on it. But overall, I don't think most people want to focus on negative motivation. In fact, I believe there are only two reasons someone would focus on negative motivation. One, they were led by fear, and they've continued the bad habits of the bad managers they grew up with. And two, negative motivation is the easy way out. Finding what will inspire someone is hard. Threatening their employment is easy. Neither of these reasons is acceptable when trying to build a culture to overcome employee disengagement.

To get you started, here are some recommended action items to help you lead with positive motivation:

- *Give employees something to run toward, not from.* In the third challenge, I addressed the need to set expectations and consequences. The importance of positive consequences was shared, and should be addressed here as well. Negative motivation gives employees something to run from. For example, if you tell an employee that the next time you catch him making a personal telephone call you will "write him up," then he very well may stop making personal telephone calls because he's afraid of getting written up. He is running from the negative consequence. (Actually, more than likely he'll continue to make personal telephone calls if he works in a culture like that. He'll just make sure he doesn't do it when you're around.) On the other hand, positive motivation gives him something to run toward. Tell him what positive thing will happen if he goes the next three months and you haven't had to talk to him about making personal telephone calls.
- *Ask employees what will inspire them.* One of the most common questions I receive is related to ways to motivate employees. Managers will tell me they've done everything they know to do, and they can't figure out how to inspire their team members. My advice to them is always the same. Stop trying to figure out what will motivate them and ask. Once you know specifically what inspires them, your efforts at motivation will work every time.
- *Focus on what employees are doing well.* The traditional performance review includes a laundry list of things needing improvement. There's nothing wrong with informing

employees of things they need to improve on, but start by telling them what they're doing well. Remember, tell them what they are doing right, then tell them how they can improve.

- *Focus on the best.* All employees are important, and deserve to be led with positive motivation. There is no group more deserving of your attention than the 29 percent at the top of your organization. These are usually the first to leave because they don't feel recognized. Identify ways to lead with positive motivation, and direct it toward those at the top.

There is a time for negative motivation, but we should start with positive motivation if we want people to do things for the right reason and if we want to build a culture to overcome employee disengagement.

CHALLENGE SIX: CELEBRATE SMALL SUCCESSES

Several years ago, I was driving down the road and saw a dog fall out of the back of a truck. I immediately turned around to make sure the dog was not hurt, and waited for the owner of the truck to return to get the dog. No one came to get the dog. Today she's mine, and her name is Bleu.

Although I didn't really want a dog at that time of my life, I was excited to have her. She was a great companion, but the fact that she wasn't trained was frustrating. So we got in the car and headed for charm school for dogs.

It was never my intention to train Bleu to do dog tricks. It was my hope that I could train her to be a good companion, not an entertainer. My motivation for training her was simple. I wanted her to sit and stay when I gave her those commands.

If you've ever trained a dog, then you know the key is repetition and reward. To that end, the instructor taught me to reward Bleu every time she made the smallest progress, and to not reward her for bad behavior. It became very obvious to me that Bleu didn't care about my ultimate goal of getting her to sit and stay. She simply wanted the consistent reward she was getting for her small accomplishments. However, the end result for recognizing all those small accomplishments was a dog that would sit and stay when commanded.

The people who work in your organization aren't all that different from Bleu. They may drool a little less and not find as much joy in chasing birds, but they do enjoy the consistent rewards for achieving small successes. My experience has shown me that most leaders are so focused on the larger goal, that the achievement of the smaller goals goes unnoticed.

Some of you may be thinking that a comparison of recognizing the performance of a dog and recognizing the performance of an employee is a little far-fetched (no pun intended). For those who think that way, I would encourage you to consider the game of football to look at how short-term successes are celebrated. There certainly is a celebration by the winning team at the end of the game. But there are many other celebrations along the way. They celebrate each time they score a touchdown, and they even celebrate each time they get a first down on the way to the touchdown.

We all set professional goals within our organization and look forward to the opportunity to celebrate the achievement of those goals. It is undeniable that if we reach our target, the achievement of the large goal was the collective achievement of many small goals. How do you celebrate those small successes within your organization?

Perhaps some leaders don't feel a need to recognize the smaller successes. I would suggest to you that the challenge is bigger than that. I believe we get so wrapped up in the pursuit of the larger vision that we often don't even recognize the achievement of the smaller successes. While we may miss the small successes, our employees seldom do, and walk away feeling underappreciated.

If you haven't made celebration a priority in the past, then it won't be an easy change to make. Allow for time in your day to seek out and celebrate these successes and recognize excellence. It keeps the team focused and moving forward, and gives them the opportunity to see the positive things happening within the organization.

To get you started, here are some recommended action items to help you celebrate small successes:

- *Create an impulsive reward system.* Employees get accustomed to established reward systems. An impulsive reward system designed specifically to celebrate small successes inspires employees to find more ways to have small successes.
- *Establish a dedicated time to celebrate every day.* When employees know that every day at a certain time the team will be brought together to celebrate successes from that specific day, they'll be inspired to find a way to be recognized. Also, celebrating with the team is important. The important thing is that every team member has the opportunity to celebrate a job well done.

- *Establish a method to celebrate every success.* In my office, we have a bell that gets rung every time we book an event. We don't ring it at the end of the day. We don't ring it once a month when we meet our monthly goal. We ring it every time we get a booking. Establish your own way to celebrate every success in your office.

Keep in mind we're talking about celebration, not just activities. I'm not talking about birthday parties and service anniversaries. These are certainly important to many employees, but those events are completely different from celebrating performance achievement. Remember, taking the time to celebrate each success will help build the momentum for more success to come.

CHALLENGE SEVEN: ENCOURAGE LIFE BALANCE FOR ALL EMPLOYEES

Once upon a time we lived in a world where employees showed up for work Monday through Friday and worked eight to nine hours then went home. There was a fine line between work life and home life. Some of you may remember those days. For most, that routine is about as realistic as a fairy tale.

Somewhere along the way the line between work and home has blurred. Some experts blame it on the Baby Boomer generation and their introduction of the twelve-hour workday. While working so hard to provide for their families and improve their lifestyles, they raised the bar in business today. Now that many of the leadership roles are held by Baby Boomers, the expectation of long hours has been passed on to the younger generations as the price of admission to the corner office.

Although some see the imbalance as a generationally driven challenge, others simply blame it on more work. We seem to live in a culture that expects people to do more with less. Organizations expect employees to step up and do more, particularly throughout the recession. For some people, there simply isn't enough time to complete the amount of work expected from employers.

For much of my career, I pursued the traditional work/life balance. Like many people in the workforce today, I viewed the pursuit of a balanced life as critical to my decision to remain with, or even join, an employer. Somewhere along the way I realized how silly it was to focus on this erroneous belief that we could ever have balance. You see, by definition, balance is an equality of distribution. The thought that we would ever have, or should ever pursue, an equal distribution between our work life and our personal life seemed nonsensical.

In my book *Living for the Weekday: What Every Employee and Boss Needs to Know about Enjoying Work and Life* (Wiley, 2010), I address the importance of changing how we view the coming together of our professional and personal lives. Instead of breaking our seven days into work and home, we should examine how the following five key aspects of life must all weave together: career, relationships, health, finances, and spirituality.

True life satisfaction (not just balance) comes when we reach our own personal level of satisfaction in each of these five areas. As employers, we must help employees understand the importance of these five areas because they all contribute to employee engagement.

As employees search for ways to weave together their career, relationships, health, finances, and spirituality, many simply want flexibility. They look around the organization and see leaders who regularly adjust their work schedules to accommodate their personal lives. In most cases, that's all any employee wants.

Managers often realize that offering flexibility is a simple way to offer life balance to all employees. Sadly, there is often a gap between flexibility in theory and the implementation of that flexibility. For flexibility to be a reality, managers must do more than just give it lip service. There must be a willingness on the part of the management team to support policies related to flexibility, and an eagerness to adjust the culture to accommodate those policies.

In many organizations, there is a direct conflict between a culture that offers life balance and a culture that expects all employees to work long and hard. For example, while technology allows us to have employees available around the clock, we can't expect them to be in "instant response" mode when they've taken time away from work for personal reasons. When these two cultures collide, life balance often has to take a backseat.

Finding a way to balance work and home in today's fast-paced world is not a simple task. For employees, it's a matter of getting the flexibility from their employer to balance all the aspects of life while putting in the work needed to advance their career. For employers, it's a matter of meeting the needs of the business while offering the flexibility. With a little effort, both sides can find a way to make it work.

To get you started, here are some recommended action items to help you encourage life balance for all employees:

- *Take advantage of technology.* While advancements in technology can often contribute to imbalance, we can take advantage of technology to help employees weave together the five aspects of their life. Years ago I had an employee who wanted to work from home two days a week. She was a new parent, and the flexibility that came from working from home was significant for her. Her job responsibilities didn't require her to be in the office to complete her work, so we took advantage of the available technology to offer her that flexibility.
- *Change your mindset.* For an employer who grew up in a world where employees came to work to do their job, the thought of allowing someone to work from home may be foreign. In the case mentioned earlier, it was difficult for me at first to envision an employee actually getting any work done outside the office. I trusted her, and I changed my mindset in order to allow the flexibility she needed to find life balance.
- *Make a list of the flexibilities you enjoy.* As a leader, you probably have flexibilities to balance your home and work life. Chances are your employees would enjoy these flexibilities, as well. To the extent their job allows it, give them some of these freedoms.
- *Protect employees' time off.* A balanced employee is a productive employee. If an employee has worked six days in a row and finally has a day off, protect that time off by allowing the employee to enjoy it. Unless it's an emergency, don't require employees to answer cell phone calls and e-mails on their day off. Although technology makes it convenient for

employees to be perpetually "on call," encourage them to spend their personal time doing personal things.

- *Set the example of life balance.* If you take a vacation, take a vacation. If you call in every few hours while you're away, you're setting an example employees think they need to follow. If you're the first person in the office and the last one to leave, you're setting an example employees think they need to follow. Be aware of the example you set.

A significant aspect of Motivational Leadership is allowing employees to find ways to weave together the five aspects of their life. Employees increasingly view the pursuit of a balanced life as critical to their decision to remain with an employer. When you provide an environment of flexibility, you increase the chances they'll stay and be engaged employees.

CHALLENGE EIGHT: CREATE A FAIR WORK ENVIRONMENT

Human resource professionals spend an abundance of their time ensuring a fair work environment. In fact, many companies have employees whose sole job is to see that the myriad of laws designed to ensure fairness are enforced. These laws are designed to guarantee employees can work in an environment free of discrimination and harassment. They are designed to ensure fair hiring practices, employee privacy, and a safe and healthy workplace.

The list of laws in place today goes on and on. I'm not a lawyer, so I'm certainly not going to provide legal advice, although I encourage you to follow all the laws required for creating a fair work environment. Not only will it keep you out of court, it will enhance your chances of developing a culture of employee engagement.

When I refer to creating a fair work environment, I'm not including what you're required by law to do. It's expected you'll do those things. Rather than the strictly legal definition of fairness, I'm referring to a fairness that engages the disengaged employee. By nature, we compare ourselves to others. We compare how much money we make to that earned by other employees. We compare what rewards we get to those awarded to other employees. We compare the attention we receive to that shown to other employees.

It is almost impossible to expect an employee to feel engaged in the workforce when she feels she hasn't been treated fairly. All too often we think we have to treat people equally, and as a result, we stop being fair.

I remember an occasion years ago where an employee asked to leave work early to attend her daughter's dance recital. When I granted the employee's request, I had a fellow manager approach me and say, "If you do that for her, you'll have to do it for everyone." I disagreed and continue to disagree today.

The next day I had some employees come to me to complain that it wasn't fair since they didn't get to leave early. When I explained that my goal was to treat people fairly, and that I would make exceptions for them when they needed it, they understood. I believe the first person who said he wanted equal treatment is the first person who didn't get fair treatment.

To get you started, here are some recommended action items to help you create a fair work environment:

- *Compensate fairly.* There may not be a law that requires you to pay one employee the same as another, but if an employee's performance is significantly better than her colleague's and she's being paid less, don't be surprised if she leaves. And don't be surprised if she stays and joins the ranks of the disengaged employees.
- *Establish equitable reward systems.* Reward systems, when used fairly, can have a tremendous impact motivating employees. Different achievements require different rewards. But if one employee reaches a milestone and the reward is a gift certificate to Outback Steakhouse, and his peer reaches the same milestone and the reward is a trip to Cancun, don't be surprised if the first employee leaves to work for your competitor.
- *Be consistent when enforcing consequences.* In the third challenge, I addressed the need to set expectations and consequences, and talked about the importance of enforcing consequences in order to drive certain behaviors. If you enforce consequences for some employees but not others, you create an environment of unfairness, and drive people toward disengagement.

Some people may say that life isn't fair, but if you want to motivate your team and build a culture to overcome employee disengagement, treat people fairly.

Organizational Leadership

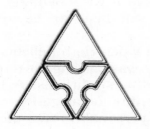

Without a clear vision for an organization, future growth is a constant challenge. Without inspired employees to help the organization pursue the vision, the journey is dull at best. But without the right team in place to make it all happen, the task of building an organization is virtually impossible.

Building the organization to make it all happen is the third and final aspect of creating a culture to overcome employee disengagement, and it's called Organizational Leadership. While Motivational Leadership focuses on the inspiration of individual employees, Organizational Leadership focuses on the development of the team. And though it is the third of the three aspects, it in no way should be considered the least important. All three leadership aspects have equal importance in developing a culture to overcome employee disengagement.

Employees come and go, even when a culture has been developed to enhance employee engagement. As employees make decisions about their future on the other side of the recession, we'll see many employees changing jobs. Some of those employees who leave will have been significant contributors to the organization. Thus, as always, we have a responsibility to cultivate a culture that will last far beyond any single person.

I remember when Herb Kelleher made the announcement he was passing the torch to new leadership at Southwest Airlines. A friend of mine thought the entire organization would change. "Without his personality and the influence he had over the culture of the airline," my friend said, "there is no way that airline will be the same."

My friend was right. There is no doubt the organization is different without Herb Kelleher involved in the day-to-day activities of the business. However, the organization didn't fundamentally change. The airline didn't close its doors. In fact, Southwest Airlines has been tremendously successful since Kelleher's departure. The leadership of that organization stepped in and continued much of what made the airline successful in the first place.

The same is true for any company that develops the team instead of focusing on individuals. If we know people will come and go, there must be an effort to build the organization so the pursuit of the vision continues.

By meeting the four challenges as outlined in this Organizational Leadership section, you can ensure a strong team is in place to carry the organization toward the vision.

CHALLENGE NINE: IDENTIFY AND POSITION THE APPROPRIATE TALENT

I've had the good fortune to work with some incredible companies over the years. Some had great teams in place, but they struggled to find the right business strategy. Others had a fine-tuned business strategy, but they lacked the talent to pull it off.

In his book *Good to Great* (HarperCollins, 2001), author Jim Collins shares what he found in organizations that were making the transformation from good to great. He says that what most organizations do is figure out where they want to go and then recruit the team. What Collins found, though, is that the leaders who took their teams from good to great first started by recruiting the right people, then decided where they wanted to go. That's a brilliant observation.

If you're in a position to be able to transform your entire organization and possibly alter the direction of the company, it's vitally important that you keep Collins's observations in mind. An organization going through complete transformation should work from that concept: build the team first, then define the vision. If, however, you are not in a position to modify your company or organization, there are realistic steps you can take to build a strong organization to pursue your existing vision.

To get you started, here are some recommended action items to help you identify and position the appropriate talent:

- *Inventory your talent.* Determine if you have the right people in the right places in your organization. In the fable, Jill was a very effective call center rep who got promoted because of her performance. She was smart enough to return to her roots when she realized management wasn't the right career for her, but many employees won't make that jump once they've settled in to a job with more pay and flexibility. If needed, move your employees around until you get them in the right position to benefit them and the company.

- *Determine who needs to go.* First of all, give the culture of employee engagement the chance to work. Once you have, determine if there are employees who need to go. Work to develop them. Work to inspire them. Once you've done everything in your power to help them and you've determined it's time for them to go, follow every procedure and law to terminate their employment.
- *Recruit the appropriate talent.* Once you've identified your needs, go out and get the right people. Don't settle for mediocrity and don't try to get off cheap. If you need a good technician, go find the best technician and pay him what he's worth. It will cost you more money in the long-run if you try to save money up front.
- *Hire for leadership needs.* A banker I met at a state banking conference told me the biggest problem he had at his bank was too many bankers. He said, "We never consider our need to fill leadership positions with good leaders. We just fill leadership positions with good bankers." Interesting point. If you need strong leadership, go find a good leader. Depending on the position you're filling, it may be easier to teach the skills needed for

that job than to teach the leadership skills needed to lead.

- *Hire for attitude.* Years ago I drove past a restaurant with a sign out front that read, "Now Hiring Smiling Faces." I remember thinking to myself, "Apparently you can have no skills at all, but as long as you're smiling, you can work for us!" Although I didn't think it was a very smart approach back then, it makes a lot of sense now. You see, you can't teach nice. You can't teach happy. But you can teach the skills that go along with the job you're filling. Start out with the right type of employee.
- *Be honest.* If you make promises you can't keep, don't be surprised when employees leave. If someone tells you the opportunity for advancement is important, don't hire her if you know there won't be opportunities for advancement because of the size or structure of the company. It's not fair to her, and it won't be fair to the company when she becomes disengaged or packs up and leaves.
- *Give challenging and meaningful work.* You've moved around your existing team to maximize their potential. You've gone out and recruited the appropriate talent. Now put them to work. Employees become disengaged when they think their potential and time are being wasted.
- *Train your employees.* Once you have them, train them. Do not assume since employees came to the table with the skills you need that you won't need to provide professional development. An untrained employee is a disengaged employee.

You can have an extraordinary vision, but if
you haven't identified and positioned the appropriate talent, all the effort and motivation in the
world won't get you there.

CHALLENGE TEN: BUILD A BRIDGE
BETWEEN GENERATIONS

My very first professional speech was on bringing
generations together in the workplace. It was titled
"Generation X in a Baby Boomer World." I had a
passion for the topic of generations back then, and
continue to have the same passion today.

Back then my interest in the topic came from
my experiences in corporate America. Every boss
I'd had was a member of the Baby Boomer generation. I am a member of Generation X. Although I
enjoyed my time in corporate America, I realized
after I was gone that my biggest challenge was
trying to live in a Baby Boomer world.

Don't get me wrong. I don't think there's anything wrong with Baby Boomers. In fact, in many
ways I am more like a Baby Boomer than an Xer.
It's just that each generation is a product of their
experiences. The Baby Boomers had different
experiences, and grew up in a different world. As
a result, we all have different expectations. When
those different expectations collide in the workplace, conflict arises.

There are many criticisms of Xers. Perhaps the
biggest is a lack of dedication. In fact, I'm frequently asked if the disengaged employees in
most organizations are from the younger generations. I believe employee disengagement is a problem across all generations, and the *Gallup
Management Journal*'s fourth national survey of
U.S. workers reinforced that belief when it showed

that the percentage of workers who say they are engaged varied only slightly by age group.

In that survey, of workers in the 18–24 age group, 35 percent indicated they were engaged. Of workers aged 25–34, 29 percent indicated they were engaged. Of workers aged 35–49, 30 percent indicated they were engaged. And for workers 50 and older, 29 percent indicated they were engaged.

Today my passion for the topic of generations continues for a different reason. When I first started as a professional speaker, I did it because I wanted to share my experiences. Now that I have worked with hundreds of clients over the years, I want to share my observations.

To get you started, here are some recommended action items to help you build a bridge between generations:

- *Understand the generations.* Do some research and learn about how each generation got the way it is. Learn what motivates them, and why they think the way they think. No two generational experts can agree on the names for the generations or the date ranges, so don't get caught up in small differences in what you read. Just keep in mind that before you can ever begin to adjust to the generations, you must understand them.
- *Suspend judgment.* We all have ideas about what each generation is like. We think some are spoiled and some are lazy. We think some aren't willing to pay their dues and feel a sense of entitlement. There may even be some truth to those accusations. But to understand people, you need to suspend judgment long enough to learn about them.

- *Don't treat everyone the same.* Once you learn about them, you'll understand why people are the way they are. You'll understand that people have different needs depending on where they are in their employment cycle, and the key to reaching them is to understand their needs in each cycle.

With multiple generations in the workforce today, an effort must be made to build a bridge between generations. It's a significant part of developing a team to realize the company's vision.

CHALLENGE ELEVEN: MOVE TOWARD REAL EMPOWERMENT

Empowerment is an amazing thing. Every employer I know wants employees who solve problems and take responsibility for their actions. In a nutshell, they want empowered employees. Every employee I know wants to be trusted and given flexibility in the way they do their job. In a nutshell, they want to be empowered employees.

While empowerment may have been a huge buzzword for the past decade or more, it is perhaps the least understood of most management practices. The concept is simple. If we give people more responsibility, then they're empowered. If we give people the power to make decisions, then they're empowered. But empowerment is so much more than that, and it is based far more on culture than on distribution of tasks.

Since empowerment is a product of an engaged culture, it takes more than a list of action items to achieve true empowerment. However, I believe there are some practical ideas I can share that will contribute to your culture of employee engagement.

To get you started, here are some recommended action items to help you move toward real empowerment:

- *Provide information.* Everyone holding this book needs information to make good decisions. As you move toward an empowered environment where employees make their own decisions, you must give them the same information you require to make sound decisions.
- *Give authority with the responsibility.* As leaders, we have both authority and responsibility (or at least we should have both). For most managers, when they give responsibility, they assume the authority goes along with it. "Give someone a task and get out of the way!" If you give them a task, ultimate success will be based on the level of authority they have to complete the task.
- *Share your power.* If you truly want employees around you to succeed in an empowered environment, then you must share your power. Most employees who have never worked in an empowered organization have never had the power to make decisions, so it's going to take a while for them to get comfortable.
- *Stop solving employees' problems.* Most employees bring problems to their bosses, looking to find someone else to make the decision. To move toward empowerment, require employees to bring you three possible solutions to any challenge they may have. Ask them which they would choose if they were making the decision, and determine if you support it. If you have good employees,

you will be amazed at how often they come up with the right solution without any help from management.

- *Get your team thinking about problems and solutions.* If there isn't much true empowerment in your organization today, your team members probably try to avoid problems. Create specific processes that reward employees for finding problems and suggesting solutions to fix them. This exercise creates a complete shift in thinking, which helps make the transition to an empowered organization.

When all is said and done, more is said than done when it comes to empowerment. It's not an easy task, but it's an essential element of success, and it is a vital piece of the puzzle of Engaged Leadership.

CHALLENGE TWELVE: ESTABLISH A STRATEGY TO MAINTAIN SUCCESS

Within each of the eleven previous challenges, I have talked about leadership tasks and management tasks. Each of these two kinds of tasks presents a range of challenges. There are those who would argue that either leadership tasks or management tasks should be of paramount importance. I'm going to skip that debate for now, but it's important to recognize that both leadership and management are important to the success of any organization.

There is no doubt that leadership and management are two different things. Leaders have a vision, a passion to pursue that vision, and a belief they can make the vision a reality. Their focus is on the future. Managers are more task-oriented.

Their focus is on the present. These are two different aspects of leading people around you, but you do not have to be two people to accomplish both aspects.

There are times when leaders will be required to do managerial things, and there are times when managers will be required to do leadership things. For this last challenge, it will require you to call on the leader in you, because this one is all about the future.

If you've ever served on the board of directors for an association or nonprofit organization, then you know the leadership changes regularly. It's nearly impossible to keep the momentum going from year to year because of turnover in board membership.

Not long ago the former president of a state association shared this story with me. A current board member of the association approached him and said, "Things were great when you were our leader. Now that you're gone, it's all fallen apart."

He explained that while he considered it a compliment that the organization worked well under his leadership, he felt he had failed to prepare the organization for the future. He said to me, "I realized I didn't establish a strategy to maintain success after I was gone. In a way, all the good I did as the president of the association was negated by the fact I didn't plan for the future."

He was right. A sign of real leadership is not what you do while you're leading an organization, but how well the organization does after you're gone.

To get you started, here are some recommended action items to help you establish a strategy to maintain success:

- *Create a succession plan.* Every organization wants to keep its best employees and continuously strengthen its team. The reality is people leave. When it's a planned departure, the transition can go relatively smoothly. However, unexpected and unpredictable departures cause some organizations to go into panic mode. Taking the time to build an organization with a culture of employee engagement and not at the same time having a succession plan makes no sense at all. Have a succession plan in place for employees at all levels.
- *Document procedures.* Every day people leave their employers and walk out the door with company assets. I'm not referring to pencils or paper clips. I'm talking about something much more valuable than office supplies. I'm referring to intellectual property. If you know of an initiative one of your employees is working on that you want repeated after that employee is gone, document the related procedures.

So much effort goes into leading an organization, as does developing a culture of employee engagement. To ensure continued success, lay a solid foundation so the organization can continue realizing its vision.

The Importance
of Character Core

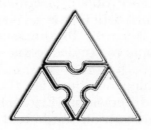

In the fable, Seth learned about the importance of character from a cab driver named Barry. Barry seemed to think someone can lack integrity in his personal life, but still have integrity in his professional life. While there may be many people who share Barry's opinion, Seth was not one of them, and neither am I. In fact, I believe there is no way to separate what you do in your private life from what you do in your professional life when it comes to character. You either have character or you don't. Period. You can't turn it on and off.

Every day you are faced with a myriad of options and opportunities. You make decisions regarding these options and opportunities based on a set of values, and if you don't have those values in place in your personal life, then you certainly don't have them in your professional life.

This leads me to the whole idea of business ethics. From time to time I will get a call from someone asking if I can do a program for their company on the topic of business ethics. With the increasing number of high-profile corporate scandals, many companies want to ensure they keep their name off the front page of the newspaper. I certainly see the problem of ethics in the workplace, but I do not believe it is an issue of business ethics. Why? Because businesses don't make decisions—people make decisions:

- Enron failed not because the organization made bad decisions. Enron failed because certain individuals made bad decisions.
- WorldCom suffered not because the organization made bad decisions. WorldCom suffered because certain individuals made bad decisions.
- Martha Stewart spent time in jail not because Martha Stewart Living Omnimedia made bad decisions. Martha Stewart spent time in jail because Martha Stewart made bad decisions.

I could fill these pages with examples of business failures, but not one of them failed because the organization made a bad decision. Every single example is the result of a person lacking personal ethics.

Leadership expert and best-selling author John C. Maxwell says it best in his book *There's No Such Thing as Business Ethics: Discover the One Rule for Making Decisions* (Faith Words, 2003). In the book, Maxwell observes: "One of our problems is that ethics is never a business issue or a social issue or a political issue. It is always a personal issue." No truer words have ever been spoken.

The leadership of any company or organization is based on the strong character of the individuals running the organization. Too many leaders today believe if they have the characteristics that make up a good leader, then character shouldn't be an issue. However, I maintain that it doesn't matter how good you are at the mechanics of leadership if the people in your organization question your character.

Employees watch their leaders much more than leaders think they do. Quite often they are looking for congruency in what we say and what we do. If we say family values are important, but we go to happy hour and begin flirting with a married coworker after enough cocktails to blur our vision, we have shown a lack of congruence in what we say and what we do. If we say that spending time with loved ones is important, but we work fourteen hours a day and most weekends while leaving family members at home alone, we have shown a lack of congruence in what we say and what we do. If we say honesty is an important value, but we ask an employee to lie to a customer by telling him we're out of the office because we're not prepared to speak with him, we have shown a lack of congruence in what we say and what we do.

I firmly believe that no one wakes up in the morning and says, "I wonder what I can do today to be unethical." But with the desire to achieve a high level of business success, many people will make unethical decisions based on their desire to get ahead. I suppose we can call this "convenience ethics," by making our decisions based on what is convenient (or profitable) at the time rather than on what is right.

I've chosen to end this book with a discussion of character because it is vital to the success of Engaged Leadership. As you can see from the model we used throughout the book, character is at the core of everything we do as Directional, Motivational, and Organizational leaders. When our employees follow us based on our strong character, we give Engaged Leadership the opportunity to work.

Conclusion

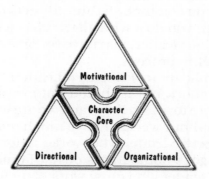

Motivational

Character Core

Directional   Organizational

What a difference four years can make! When the first edition of *Engaged Leadership* was released in 2007, organizations were focused on employee engagement to help them *thrive*. Today, organizations are focused on employee engagement to help them *survive*. Regardless of your motive, it ultimately all comes down to leadership.

As I travel around the world speaking, I am constantly amazed at how receptive people are to learning about leadership. My experience has been that people are absolutely exhausted with being managed and they are utterly starved for being led.

I truly believe the concepts presented in *Engaged Leadership* are what people are looking for today. They were looking for it four years ago, and they're still looking for it. They want to understand, and be a part of, the bigger picture and long-term vision. You can provide that with Directional Leadership. They want to be inspired to pursue that long-term vision. You can provide that with Motivational Leadership. They want to be a part of a strong, productive team. And you can provide that with Organizational Leadership.

When you combine all three aspects of Engaged Leadership, and do it with all the character needed to be seen as a leader, you have become engaged in the leadership process.

The application of Engaged Leadership takes a dedicated effort, but it should not mean you need to work more to attain it. In fact, we are working too many sixty-hour weeks. I have much more respect for the effective leader who works a normal work-week and goes home to his or her family than an ineffective leader who must work sixty hours to do what others can accomplish in forty hours.

Above all, I believe people are looking for someone to express optimism for the future. They want leaders who don't let obstacles stop them. They want leaders to keep hope alive. The time is right for enthusiasm. It is my hope that you seize the moment.

The Employee's Role

A s I travel around and speak on the topic of Engaged Leadership, I am often asked about the employee's role in employee engagement. With three out of four employees at some level of disengagement, it seems fair to assume the employee should play a role in a culture of employee engagement.

In this book I have addressed the leader's responsibility to create a culture where employees want to work. But to maximize a culture of engagement, employees must be responsible for showing up with a certain level of personal engagement. Without a doubt, employee engagement is a two-way road.

To address the employee's role, I wrote a follow-up to this book; it's titled *Living for the Weekday: What Every Employee and Boss Needs to Know about Enjoying Work and Life* (Wiley, 2010). In that book, I address the five aspects of life all employees should be working to weave together: career, relationships, health, finances, and spirituality. Each of these is important because they affect each other, and ultimately, they affect an employee's ability to be engaged.

Employees benefit personally when they find a way to weave together these five aspects of their life, and leaders benefit as well. You see, the leader can do everything outlined in *Engaged Leadership* and yet not create an engaged culture if the employees aren't doing their part. For instance, the leader can ensure an employee understands clearly the role he or she plays in an organization, but it won't matter if the employee isn't "there" because of a poor relationship with his or her spouse. The leader can create incredible reward systems to recognize superior performance, but it won't matter if employees aren't "there" because they are trying to figure out how to pay the bills because they have done a lousy job managing personal finances. The leader can empower employees to take on greater responsibility, but it won't matter if employees aren't "there" because a lack of focus on their physical and/or emotional health causes them to lose focus on the job at hand.

To show the direct link between the leader's role and the employee's role, in the new book I have retold the fable from *Engaged Leadership* from the perspective of the employee. This time, I tell the fable through the eyes of Miles Freeman, one of Seth's employees who struggles with the disengagement of everyone around him. With the help of some insightful and timely training on life balance, Miles discovers that employee engagement is the result of some specific choices he and his coworkers make in their personal lives.

When both leaders and employees are doing their part, employee engagement has the potential to go to a whole new level. *Living for the Weekday* can help you address the employee's role in employee engagement by getting people to look forward to Monday as much as they look forward to Friday.

ACKNOWLEDGMENTS

Anyone who has taken on the task of writing a book knows it's a collaborative effort. I have had the benefit of the generous guidance and encouragement of many people, and would like to extend my deepest gratitude and sincere appreciation to the following people who helped make this book possible with their great ideas, endless encouragement, and timely support.

I want to start by thanking my wife Heather. You make my life such a fun and meaningful adventure. I appreciate your unconditional love, understanding, and commitment. You make all that I do worthwhile.

To my mother, Sherron Hartin: The sacrifices you've made for me helped me become the man I am today, and I will be eternally grateful to you.

To my family and friends: For the support and encouragement along the way. I'm often asked if I have a favorite place to travel, and my answer is always the same. Home. No matter where I travel in the world, I always know I can return home to my family and friends. Much of my life is spent on the road away from the people who mean so much to me, and I want you all to know the appreciation I have for the interest you've shown in my career. If I attempted to list individual names, I know I'd leave someone out. You know who you are, and I appreciate you more than you can ever imagine.

And I want to send special thanks to my family at St. Paul Lutheran Church of Bulverde. There is perhaps no more important work than the work I do with you. You keep me grounded and provide the motivation to continue doing my thing, and I appreciate you for that.

These acknowledgments would not be complete if I did not recognize and thank my two college mentors who helped lead me in the direction of leadership development: David Hartz, who saw potential in a young man and put me on my first stage, and Earl Moseley, who shared that stage with me and taught me a great deal about the importance of character. After a long and hard-fought battle with cancer, Earl was called home this past year. I am a better man today for having had him in my life, and I will be forever grateful for the many life lessons he shared over the years. Godspeed, Earl Moseley!

A huge thank-you goes to the many associations and corporations that have included my programs in their meetings or training events. While it has been an honor to share my thoughts on personal and professional leadership enhancement, it has been a learning experience every step of the way. My life is a classroom, and thanks to your confidence in me, I have been able to learn from each and every one of you.

Thanks also go to my bosses, peers, and employees throughout my professional career. So many of you were great leaders and taught me many of the concepts I discuss in this book. Also, thanks to the few of you who served as a miserable excuse for a leader. While it's important to learn what to do from great leaders, it's equally valuable to learn what not to do from lousy ones. No need for names . . . you know who you are.

Thanks to the entire team at John Wiley & Sons, Inc., for your expertise and contributions to this book, especially my editor Laurie Harting. Your interest in me helped get the first edition in the hands of people I have never met. To my new editor, Shannon Vargo, who has made this second edition a reality. And to Elana Schulman, Kim Dayman, and Lauren Freestone for all you do.

And saving the most important for last, I thank God for the talents to do His good work through me. It is my hope that one day I will look my maker in the face and hear the words, "Well done, my good and faithful servant. Well done." I hope I've made Him proud.

ABOUT THE AUTHOR

Clint Swindall is the president and CEO of Verbalocity, Inc., a personal development company with a focus on leadership enhancement. These solutions include leadership enhancement programs, training, speaking, and general consulting.

After a successful corporate career that included time in the Leadership Development Program at SBC Communications (now AT&T), Clint chose to pursue his true passion of changing lives and helping people enhance their personal and professional leadership skills. Since founding Verbalocity a decade ago, Clint has dedicated his time to helping organizations overcome the challenge of employee disengagement.

Clint enjoys the challenge of enhancing the leadership experiences of his clients by delivering programs based on *Engaged Leadership: Building a Culture to Overcome Employee Disengagement*. He recognizes that a culture of employee engagement is a two-way road, and that true engagement comes when leaders and employees are both doing their part. In addition to working with leaders to build a culture to overcome employee disengagement, Clint addresses the employee's role in his follow-up book *Living for the Weekday: What Every Employee and Boss Needs to Know about Enjoying Work and Life*.

Clint travels the world delivering high-content speeches and training in an entertaining and inspirational style to Fortune 500 companies, government agencies, and trade associations. His clients include 7-Eleven, American Express, BMW, Hallmark Gold Crown, Valero Energy Corporation, Enterprise Rent-a-Car, Uno Chicago Grill, and Keller Williams Realty.

Clint is a recipient of the Certified Speaking Professional designation. Less than 10 percent of speakers worldwide who belong to the National Speakers Association and the International Federation for Professional Speakers earn this designation. As a professional speaker, trainer, and leadership consultant, he has delivered his programs throughout the United States, Canada, South America, Mexico, Bermuda, and The Bahamas.

Clint lives with his wife, Heather, in Bulverde, Texas, just north of San Antonio in the Texas Hill Country where they are raising their three "girls"— Black, Bleu, and Bailey (their three dogs)!